THE
HEALED
SOUL

BY ELLASIN D. ALLEN, MS, LPC

THE HEALED SOUL

Published by

iPress Publishing

Newport News, Virginia

www.ipresspublishing.com

Unless otherwise indicated, all Scripture quotations are taken from the **King James Version (KJV)** of the Holy Bible.

Printed in the United States of America

For more information or for bulk purchases, please visit

www.ipresspublishing.com

ISBN: 978-1-969504-05-1

Cover design by **iPress Publishing**

Interior design by **Tessy Odigi**

iPress
PUBLISHING

DEDICATION

*To my Lord and Savior, Jesus Christ, the Restorer
of my soul and the One who transformed my
broken pieces into something beautiful. Every page
of this book stands as a witness to Your grace, Your
healing power, and Your unfailing love that made
me whole.*

*To my husband, Pastor Eric L. Allen, thank you
for carrying me through the dark seasons and
celebrating me in the light. Your love, covering,
and unwavering support helped me rise in
moments when I wanted to fall. Thank you for
believing in the woman I was becoming. Your love
lifted me, your faith strengthened me, and your
presence reminded me that healing is not only
possible—it is promised.*

*To my children, Chalanna, Darius, and Ayshia—
each of you holds a sacred place in my heart.
Thank you for your understanding, love, and
compassion throughout my healing journey. You
are my joy, my inspiration, and one of the greatest
reasons I chose to heal.*

FOREWORD

There are few journeys more profound than the journey toward healing. It is a sacred path that asks us to confront our pain, rediscover our worth, and reclaim our peace. In *The Healed Soul*, Ellasin Allen invites us to walk that path with courage and authenticity, offering not only insight but her lived experience. This book is more than words on a page; it is a companion for anyone who longs to be whole again.

As Ellasin's mentor, I have had the privilege of witnessing her transformation firsthand. I've seen how the lessons within these chapters were not born from theory, but from real moments of struggle, surrender, and grace. What you hold in your hands is the fruit of deep reflection and divine restoration, a testimony that healing is possible for every soul willing to seek it.

Each page carries an invitation: to slow down, to listen inwardly, and to allow truth to do its quiet, powerful work. You will find yourself reflected in these words, and perhaps, by the end, you will recognize that the healing you seek has been within reach all along.

May this book meet you where you are and remind you that brokenness is not the end of your story. It is, in fact, the beginning of a beautiful new chapter, the story of a healed soul.

Dr. D. Moore, LPC-S
Mentor & Friend

THE HEALED SOUL

*"In Christ, the wounds that once defined us become the
very soil where grace blossoms."*

ELLASIN D. ALLEN, M.S., LPC

Founder of Journey Psychotherapy | Author of The Healed Soul

M y journey toward healing began long
before I became a Licensed Mental Health
Counselor. I grew up in an environment
marked by domestic violence and abuse,
experiences that left deep emotional wounds and shaped how
I viewed love, safety, and worth. For years, I survived through
silence and learned to disconnect from my pain, a psychological
defense known as dissociation. It was my way of coping when
life felt unbearable.

Through therapy, faith, and reflection, I began to understand that what I once accepted as love was not love at all. Healing required me to confront my past, challenge the lies I believed about myself, and rediscover my identity in God. I learned that true love begins with Him and flows through self-awareness, self-respect, and compassion. That revelation transformed not only my life but my calling.

Today, as the founder of *Journey Psychotherapy* and author of *The Healed Soul*, I help others bridge the gap between faith and mental health. My passion is to walk with individuals as they uncover the roots of their pain and find restoration for their souls. I believe healing is not just possible, it's promised. My mission is to help others live whole, live free, and begin where the healing of the soul truly starts.

A MESSAGE FROM MY HEART

This is not your typical self-help book. In 2020, God spoke to me clearly: *"It's time to share your story."* At first, I did not understand the weight of that instruction. Over the past few years, I have used my voice, my platforms, and my experiences to speak the truth, offer healing, and share hope, but at the close of 2024, God spoke again. This time, His words carried both urgency and compassion: *"My sons and daughters are silently hurting. I need you to tell your testimony. In you is someone's hope, someone's deliverance. Let them know that there is healing and joy in Me, and that life is still worth living."*

This book is the result of that divine assignment. Within these pages, you will find pieces of my own journey, the moments of pain, confusion, surrender, and restoration that shaped me into the woman I am today. Every word is written from my heart to yours, to remind you that you are not alone.

We are going to feel, deal, and heal together. Along the way, we will shed tears, share laughter, and discover the unshakable peace of God that truly surpasses all understanding. My prayer is that as you read, something in you awakens, the courage to face your truth, the grace to forgive yourself, and the faith to believe that your story, too, can be redeemed.

So, friend, let us walk this journey together, toward wholeness, freedom, and the best version of who God created you to be.

CONTENTS

INTRODUCTION

As I sit here with tears in my eyes, reminiscing over my life, how much of an oxymoron it was. From the outside, it appeared to be good. We had a big yellow 3-story house, with a fence, a big yard, and a dog. I went to a private school. You know the American dream, right? The neighborhood was beautiful; at any given moment, you would see kids playing double Dutch, hopscotch, or kick the can. The neighbors lived by the concept that it takes a village to raise a child; the older kids watched out for us. Oh, what fun times we had. When my siblings and I lived at home, we would have family barbecues, and I remember that we had one room that we called the music room.

Everyone would gather in there, crowding around the record player. We would listen to Smokey Robinson, The Four Tops, Marvin Gaye, and Barry White. And other songs like "Used to be my girl" and "Brick House," y'all get the picture. I loved Christmas because we would have the big ol' Christmas tree right by the wooden fireplace, along with other decorations.

Outside, we would have Santa and the reindeer on the roof, Frosty the Snowman in front, and our house would be lit up like something you would see in the movies.

That was from the outside looking in. I grew up in an era where the thing was "what goes on in this house stays in this house," which made living inside a different story. The walls can't talk, so it leaves me to tell a story. When the company was gone, the lights turned down, and the music stopped playing, that is when the gates of hell opened. I have numerous memories of the emotional, mental, physical, sexual, and financial abuse that transpired for years. If that is not enough, to this day, I can close my eyes and visions are vivid as if it were just yesterday.

Although I cry, although I see and still have the memories, they no longer control me.

Childhood trauma has multifaceted effects that extend into adulthood, influencing psychological health, brain development, behavior, and societal functioning. If you can address these impacts through early intervention, trauma-informed care, and preventive strategies is crucial for individual recovery and societal well-being. Unfortunately, most of us are unaware that we are broken. Our dysfunctional environment has become our norm and impacts us as adults and in our relationships.

What is trauma? It took me three counselors and for me to get my degree to be able to recognize I lived a traumatic life, and two to articulate that I lived a traumatic life. Today, I can say I survived and healed from my trauma. Now, what is trauma, and what does it cause?

Understanding Trauma

Trauma is the emotional response to an event or experience that overwhelms an individual's ability to cope. It can stem from physical or emotional abuse, neglect, loss, accidents, natural disasters, or witnessing violence. Trauma does not discriminate; it affects people regardless of age, gender, or background. It is crucial to recognize that trauma is subjective and deeply personal; an experience that may be traumatic for one individual might not be perceived in the same way by another.

As a Licensed Professional Counselor, I can tell you that psychologically, trauma activates the brain's survival mode, particularly the amygdala, which governs fear responses. This can result in hypervigilance, flashbacks, nightmares, emotional numbness, and difficulties with trust. Chronic trauma can also lead to Post Traumatic Stress Disorder (PTSD). Being diagnosed, I can now say that it is characterized by long-term emotional dysregulation and disturbed self-identity. Unfortunately, many of us do not seek help, or our environment does not change, so we never deal with it. We throw our hands up and say, "It is what it is," but I am here to tell you it is not. There are consequences of unhealed trauma.

The Impact of Unhealed Trauma

Unhealed trauma manifests in various ways: anxiety, depression, addiction, difficulty in relationships, self-sabotaging behaviors, and even physical illnesses. People with unresolved trauma often develop coping mechanisms that initially offer relief but later prove harmful, such as emotional detachment or substance abuse. Left unaddressed, trauma can perpetuate cycles of pain across generations, particularly within families and communities.

Moreover, trauma affects not just memory but perception. Survivors may develop distorted beliefs about themselves ("I am unlovable") or the world ("People are dangerous"), leading to isolation and hopelessness. Recognizing these patterns is a crucial step in the healing process.

Listen, my brothers and sisters, you have generations that are coming after you that are depending on you getting healed. That depends on you to be whole. It is time to end generational curses and start the rise of generational blessings. Amen somebody.

In writing this book, I pray that when the last chapter is complete, you will no longer be in bondage to what people said about or have done to you. You will no longer feel guilty or carry the consequences of someone else's actions. I pray you will not hold yourself hostage to the bad decisions you made. We've been dying long enough; it is time to bloom from the hurt within. It's time to be a Healed Soul. And we are going to do that in steps. Take your time, this is not a sprint but a marathon. Let me put it this way. Have you ever asked yourself how a toddler can move so fast with those tiny legs? Because they don't stop. This is your journey.

Healing is not a destination but a lifelong journey. Triggers may still appear, and difficult emotions may resurface. However, with time and commitment, these moments become more manageable. What once felt like a shattering experience may transform into a source of resilience and empathy.

Importantly, healing is not about becoming who you were before the trauma; it's about becoming who you are now, fully and authentically. Survivors are not defined by what happened to them, but by how they choose to reclaim their lives.

Healing from past trauma is one of the most challenging and courageous journeys a person can undertake. It demands self-awareness, vulnerability, and persistence. Though the scars of trauma may never completely disappear, they need not dictate the future. With the right tools, support, and mindset, healing is not only possible but can also become a pathway to deeper understanding, connection, and personal transformation.

I am not writing this for pity. I was kept for a purpose. I am writing this because the pain I walked through became the platform for my purpose. The very things that tried to break me are the reason I can speak with such conviction today. My story isn't one of defeat; it's a testimony of God's strength and faithfulness.

I am not my pain, and pain is not my portion; victory is. Every tear, every trial, every moment I thought I would not make it was shaping me for this very moment. My suffering gave me compassion. My brokenness gave me language for other broken hearts. Now, I can look someone in the eyes and say, *"If you don't give up, if you hold on to your faith, God will restore you."*

I will never forget the words of the therapist who walked beside me during my healing journey. She looked at me one day and said, *"It's a wonder you're not in a mental institution."* And she was right. By all natural accounts, I should not be here, in my right mind, with peace in my heart. But I know, I was kept by God. Preserved on purpose. Sustained by grace.

For such a time as this, I am here to remind you: if He kept me, He can keep you, too. For every survivor, let me make this clear: you are not alone, your pain is real, and healing is within reach.

May God bless and keep you while you are on your journey to healing.

CHAPTER
One
STAINED
AND
TAINTED

I was shattered before I developed. My innocence was robbed, my early childhood was tainted, my middle childhood was destroyed, and from my adolescence to early adulthood, I thought my body was my voice. How did I get here?! These are some of my stories.

I grew up in an environment marked by domestic violence, an atmosphere where I not only witnessed abuse but also became a victim of it. My childhood innocence was stolen far too early when a family member decided that a five-year-old child could serve his distorted sense of pleasure. I remember trying to protect myself the only way I knew how, placing obstacles and makeshift traps around my bed, hoping it would keep him away. What stands out most, even now, is that no one ever asked why he was in my room to begin with.

The silence in my home was deafening. When the people who are supposed to protect you look the other way, it teaches you to do the same, to look away from your own pain. I learned to be quiet, not because I did not want to speak, but because my voice had already been dismissed. People often ask, *"Why didn't you tell someone?"* But how do you tell when the very people you would have told made you feel invisible, like the family's black sheep, a mistake they regretted, an inconvenience they tolerated? How do you cry out for help when you've been conditioned to believe that your feelings don't matter?

The truth is, I did not have a voice because no one ever showed me that mine was worth hearing.

Adding to the confusion of my childhood, when I was ten years old, my sister and I spent the night at her friend's house. I had only met the woman once and had never met her daughter. What should have been a simple sleepover turned into yet another moment that added another layer to the dysfunctional life I was secretly living. The lady's daughter, roughly five years my senior, came into the room and had sexual relations with me. To this day, I can still see the room vividly in my mind, every detail, every shadow.

What grieves me most is that I did not move, I did not speak, I just lay there in silence. Somewhere deep inside, I already knew the routine. Sadly, this kind of violation had become familiar. I had learned early on that my safety did not matter and that my voice carried no weight. After all, who cared about me? I did not feel protected by anyone.

I wish I could say that was the last time I experienced sexual abuse, but it was not. Each incident left another scar, both seen and unseen. By that point, dissociation had become my survival strategy. It was the only way I knew how to cope with the unbearable pain. I had learned to detach from what was happening to me, to escape into a place in my mind where I did not have to feel. It was not a choice but a necessity, a way to protect my mind from an emotional reality that was too painful to process at such a young age. Over time, pretending became so normal that I struggled to tell the difference between what was real and what was not.

Professional Moment

Dissociation is a psychological response that often occurs when an individual experiences overwhelming trauma, including sexual trauma. It is the mind's way of protecting itself from unbearable pain, fear, or violation by creating a sense of separation from reality, emotions, or even the body. When a person experiences something deeply distressing or life-threatening, the brain may "disconnect" to create distance from the experience, almost as if watching it happen from outside of themselves. This can manifest as feeling numb, detached, or disconnected from one's body and surroundings. While dissociation can be a survival mechanism in the moment of trauma, it can later disrupt daily life, relationships, and self-awareness, leaving individuals struggling to feel present or grounded. Let me put it another way, unfortunately, many people act this way, often appearing emotionless, and do not understand why there is a disconnect between them, their emotions, and their loved ones.

When dissociation arises from sexual trauma, it often stems from the body and mind's attempt to survive a profoundly violating experience. Dissociation becomes a means of coping with feelings of shame, violation, and powerlessness. Survivors may experience flashbacks, blackouts, or fragmented memories of the event because their minds shielded them from the full intensity of what occurred. Some people may also have difficulty feeling safe in their own bodies, sometimes describing themselves as "shutting down" or "going somewhere else" during the trauma. While this response may have protected the individual during the traumatic event, ongoing dissociation can interfere with intimacy and trust. It's important as a survivor to understand at the time, utilizing dissociation was a protective response rather than a weakness. This can help individuals reframe their experiences with compassion and is an important step toward recovery and integration.

Sheesh, this was a lot and may have been triggering for some of you. Let us take a moment to feel, deal with, and heal together. I want you to take a few deep breaths and, as you exhale, release those emotions associated with the trigger. Repeat after me, I am not my past. I no longer have to feel ashamed of other people's actions or the negative decisions that I made. This next part is important. You must reflect on what you have overcome and accomplished. It is important to see your progress, or you will stay stuck in your past.

Listen, if at any time it becomes too much, please put the book down

My Body as My Voice.

Yes, I said it, my body was my voice.

I say that because when those individuals decided to steal my innocence, something inside me shifted. It felt as though I had a target on my back that silently told the world it was acceptable to use, abuse, and mistreat me. Almost every relationship I entered during my unhealed years carried some form of pain, whether emotional, mental, physical, or sexual.

Sadly, like many others, I believed this was simply my life. I accepted dysfunction as normal because I did not know what healthy looked like.

What I did not realize then was that those horrific experiences were shaping my definition of love. I began to equate sexual desire with love and affection. If someone wanted me sexually, I thought it meant they cared for me. And if they did not want me, I assumed something was wrong with me. That mindset became my downfall. It led me into situationships, entanglements, and relationships that only deepened my brokenness.

What hurt the most, though, were the judgments from others, the whispers and labels. People would say things like, *"She's too grown," "She's fast,"* or *"She's hot in the pants."* And for the boys, it was, *"He's so angry,"* or *"He just stays to himself."* But rarely did anyone stop to ask *why* a child would act out or withdraw, or what pain might be hiding behind those behaviors. Instead of compassion, we were met with criticism. Instead of safety, we were met with shame.

Can I talk to the ladies for a moment? Fellas, hold on, you're next.

Ladies, if no one ever told you, or if you never believed it, your body is precious. Our bodies hold profound significance, not only as vessels of life and creation but also as symbols of strength, resilience, and identity. It is through a woman's body that generations are birthed, nurtured, and sustained, reflecting the divine ability to create and care. There is a book by Dr. Bessel Van Der Kolk entitled "The Body Keeps Score." If you haven't read it, I highly recommend it. It is my understanding that beyond its biological functions, a woman's body carries her lived experiences, emotions, and cultural identity, shaping how she interacts with the world and how the world responds to her. One of my favorite sayings is We teach people how to treat us. That is why recognizing the importance of our bodies means respecting our autonomy, protecting our well-being, and affirming our right to feel safe, valued, and empowered in every space we occupy.

Now, Fellas, listen, I know this is a sensitive topic, but we all need some help. Your bodies are just as important. Because A man's body is important not only for its physical strength and endurance but also as a vessel that carries his purpose, emotions, and identity. Do I need to repeat that?! You are somebody; it is time to let go of what they said and what they didn't do. It is through your body that you engage with the world, working, protecting, providing, and nurturing in your unique ways. Just like women, men's bodies deserve respect, care, and recognition, as you often silently bear the weight of societal expectations and emotional burdens. Ladies, honoring the importance of a man's body includes encouraging him to prioritize his health, creating a safe place for him to express his feelings, and breaking free from harmful stereotypes that equate strength with silence. Men, your body reflects your humanity, deserving dignity, rest, and the freedom to be whole.

Unfortunately, this story is relatable to too many young women and men. Some will never tell; for others, they learned early on that their voices do not matter. They won't seek help professionally or spiritually. So, we go through life slowly dying inside, aimlessly searching for a version of love, and starving for a glimpse of hope.

When a person experiences trauma, including sexual trauma, it can deeply impact a person's sense of self, relationships, and boundaries. For me, I had no boundaries, which led to being promiscuous. I had the dysfunctional thought that you are not going to take my body, so I will give it away. This made me feel like I was in control. Let me explain. For some survivors, that is what we are: we are not victims. For some survivors, promiscuity may develop as a coping mechanism to regain a sense of control over their bodies and experiences. Because trauma often leaves individuals feeling powerless or violated, engaging in frequent or casual sexual encounters can sometimes be an unconscious attempt to reclaim autonomy or redefine intimacy on their own terms. For me and maybe you, promiscuity served as both a shield and a search for validation, offering temporary relief from feelings of shame, worthlessness, or emotional numbness.

For some, unresolved trauma can distort the way a person understands love, safety, and attachment. Some individuals may seek connection through sexual activity, mistaking physical closeness for emotional intimacy, or they may use sex to escape painful memories and emotions. Let me help you; this behavior is not about moral character, but rather about the lingering wounds that shape one's choices and needs. While promiscuity may temporarily soothe feelings of emptiness or help mask emotional pain, for me and even some of you, it left us feeling unfulfilled or even retraumatized.

There were times I would be mentally and emotionally spiraling because of shame and guilt. Guilt and shame are heavy burdens and are often carried by individuals who have survived sexual assault or abuse. I, just like many survivors, internalized the false belief that the abuse was our fault, blaming ourselves for not fighting back, for being vulnerable, or for somehow "causing" the abuse. Shame, unlike guilt, reaches even deeper. I, just like other survivors, was convinced that something was fundamentally wrong or broken within me. Clinically speaking, these distorted beliefs are often reinforced by societal stigma, victim-blaming attitudes, or silence surrounding sexual violence. As a result, survivors may struggle with self-worth, feeling unworthy of love, respect, or happiness, just like I did.

I did not know that true happiness came from within; I was looking for everyone else to make me happy. Little did I know that my unresolved feelings of guilt and shame had a profound effect on my relationships. How? I'm glad you asked. Survivors may find it difficult to trust others, fearing judgment, rejection, or betrayal if their past is revealed. Intimacy can be especially challenging; physical closeness may trigger memories of the abuse, causing anxiety, discomfort, or avoidance of sexual relationships altogether. On the other hand, some may overcompensate by seeking approval through people-pleasing behaviors or by tolerating unhealthy relationships because they feel undeserving of something better. These struggles can create cycles of pain that reinforce the shame many survivors already carry.

Shame and guilt can have a long-term impact and can manifest in many areas of life, romantic relationships, parenting, work, and even faith. Some people may live with an ongoing inner critic, battling feelings of inadequacy or self-sabotage. Oh, self-sabotaging, sigh, we will talk about that later. However, a good book to read is "The Mountain Is You" by Brianna Wiest. I use this with clients that display certain behaviors, and yesssss I read it and applied it. Where were we, oh yes, self-sabotaging can lead to difficulties setting healthy boundaries, maintaining confidence, or pursuing personal goals. Without proper healing, guilt and shame can keep individuals trapped in silence, preventing them from reclaiming their voice and sense of identity. However, with therapy, support systems, and self-compassion, survivors can begin to challenge those false beliefs, release misplaced guilt, and transform shame into resilience, allowing them to thrive in relationships and in life.

REFLECTIVE *Questions*

1. In what ways has silence, whether self-imposed or conditioned by others, shaped the way you see yourself, your worth, and your ability to speak truth about your pain?

    ....

    ....

    ....

    ....

2. How have your past experiences of trauma or invalidation influenced the way you define love, safety, and control, and what would reclaiming your voice and redefining those meanings look like for you today?

    ....

    ....

    ....

    ....

CHAPTER
Two

THE OUTSIDER IN
THE FAMILY

L osing (I will share my pet peeve about this word later) one's sense of self is one of the deepest wounds that can come from experiencing domestic violence or sexual assault at a young age. When trauma happens during those formative years, it interrupts the natural process of identity development. Instead of learning who you are through safety, love, and guidance, you begin to define yourself through pain, fear, and survival. I remember feeling as though pieces of me were taken away: my innocence, my voice, and my confidence. It was as if the person I might have grown into had been stolen before I had the chance to discover her. For many survivors, this is the reality: they grow up believing they are what happened to them, rather than recognizing the truth of their worth and potential.

Professional Moment

From a therapeutic perspective, this disconnection from self is both a survival mechanism and a source of long-term struggle. As children, survivors often adapt by silencing their own needs, ignoring their feelings, or even blaming themselves for the abuse. Over time, these coping strategies can cause them to lose touch with their authentic selves. Instead of seeing their value, they may view themselves through the eyes of their abuser, feeling unworthy, ashamed, or invisible.

As adults, this loss of identity often carries into relationships, work, and even faith. Survivors may struggle with boundaries, self-doubt, or the fear of being truly seen. It can feel as though life is lived in fragments, with parts of the self-locked away for protection. I can recall moments when I did not even recognize myself, when I would question, *Who am I beyond this pain?* That is the hidden wound of trauma: it convinces you that your identity has been erased, when in reality, it has only been buried.

Can I talk about my pain for a moment? Thank you. My story did not just begin at birth; it began in pain long before I took my first breath. I was conceived in pain, carried in pain, and born through pain. My father beat my mother while she was pregnant with me. Out of hatred for him, one of my siblings even punched her in the stomach while I was still in the womb. My mother endured physical, emotional, and mental suffering in bringing me into the world. She once told me herself that she drank a fifth of rum right before giving birth to me. I carried that knowledge with me my entire life, haunted by questions I could never answer: Did she drink because she did not want to feel the pain of bringing a child into a broken and dysfunctional relationship? Did she drink because of the hell she knew she was going to endure, always attached to this demonic man because of me? Or did she drink out of regret? Whatever the reason, her pain became my pain, physically, mentally, and emotionally.

Mentally, I was scarred by the words spoken over me. I can still hear the names I was called: "You're ugly. You look just like your father. You are the darkest one in the family. Bald-headed." I remember when I was in middle school, there was a boy I liked, and I heard he was going to ask me out. I asked my sister to do my hair, and something went wrong. I still do not know what happened, but I ended up having to cut all my hair off. My siblings laughed at me, and I cried myself to sleep. I stopped eating, I did not want to be around anyone, and looking back, I realized that I was battling depression. That Monday, when I went to school, thank God no one made fun of me, but needless to say, the boy never asked me out. That was my first heartbreak, and it cut deeper than just a school crush; it confirmed the lies I had already been told about myself.

Physically, my life was marked by violence. My father's anger toward my mother often spilled onto me and my siblings. He would throw me against the wall, knock me down, and beat me to hurt her. When I was just five years old, he beat me so badly that I almost lost my life. My siblings, also shaped by that environment of abuse, turned their pain on me, too. I endured black eyes, punches, beatings, and emotional abuse. I know now they act out of what they saw and the hatred they felt toward my father. But as a child, all I understood was rejection and pain. That pain carried over into my body, my health, and later, into many of my relationships.

I keep saying my father because I was the only one who was his child. That can pose a problem. For a brief moment, venture with me as I side-track.

When you are the only child in a household with a different parent than your siblings, that difference can create a division you did not ask for and do not know how to fix. Especially in blended families, dynamics become complicated quickly. And when the new parent is controlling, mean, or abusive, that pain multiplies, and the child without shared biological ties often bears the brunt of it.

It is not always the case, but let us tell the truth, it *can* happen. I have lived it.

Sometimes, the parent who marries in does not see the "stepchild" as their own. And even if they never say it aloud, it shows in their actions: the harsh tone, the stricter rules, the colder stare, the lack of warmth. But what hurts just as much, maybe even more, is when your own siblings, the ones who share your blood, join in the rejection. They mirror the behavior of the abusive parent. They take their cues from the one in power. And suddenly, you are alone in a house full of people.

When You're the Child of "The Other Parent"

Also, being the only child from a previous relationship can be a silent trauma. You carry the history of a parent no one else shares, and sometimes no one respects. The new parent might constantly compare you, criticize you, or emotionally alienate you. And if the biological parent does not intervene, the child begins to internalize the message: *I'm the problem.*

According to recent studies, children in stepfamilies are at higher risk for emotional and behavioral challenges, particularly when the stepparent-child relationship is marked by conflict, neglect, or abuse (Ganong & Coleman, 2017). These children often report feeling less supported, less protected, and more like outsiders in their own home.

As you grow older, the wounds from a fractured family do not disappear; they evolve. Children from blended homes with unresolved trauma often struggle with:

- Trust issues

- Chronic people-pleasing

- Identity confusion

- Fear of abandonment

- Internalized shame

You may constantly seek validation in relationships or question your worth in spaces where you do not feel fully accepted. But the truth is, *you never had to earn the love you deserved as a child.* It was your birthright. You just were not given it.

Discovering Me

This is only a glimpse of what I have endured, but I need to pause here. My story does not end in pain; it ends in purpose.

Okay, wipe your tears, shake off the disbelief, and let's get back to Discovering Me.

In discovering who you are after uncovering all that life has covered you with, it is essential to know that healing invites survivors to slowly uncover who they are beneath the trauma. Through therapy, faith, and supportive relationships, I learned that my voice still existed, that my dreams still mattered, and that my worth had never been destroyed. Reclaiming identity after abuse is not easy; it is a journey of courage, patience, and self-compassion. But with time, survivors can rediscover themselves, not defined by victimhood, but empowered by resilience, ready to live authentically and fully.

I heard you. How? One decision at a time. Choices are given and decisions are made. If you are ready to feel, deal, and heal, then you can take back control of yourself.

Repeat after me: "I Choose ME!" Yes, you declared it, and now it's time to walk in it. But what does that really mean? And who is *ME*? Let me remind you, *you are not your past, and you are not lost.* Too many times, I hear people say, "I'm a lost cause." But I ask, lost where? What "lost and found" are you at, so I can come get you? The Word of God tells us that He leaves the ninety-nine to go after the one, so even if you feel lost, Heaven knows exactly where you are. Let me repeat it with authority: You. Are. Not. Lost.

Life will "life," and trials will come. Circumstances can pile up, adding layer upon layer until you can barely recognize yourself. But God sees you through the blood of Jesus, not through the dirty lens of life. You are not forgotten; you are planted. Just like a seed hidden in the ground, it may look buried, but in reality, it is being prepared for growth. In

God's timing, those layers of dirt will give way to new life, new purpose, and new strength. You are not a mistake; you are chosen, called, and equipped to bloom into everything God created you to be.

Just like a seed must first take root in the soil, you too must grow strong spiritual roots. The deeper those roots go, the stronger and more firmly grounded the tree, bush, or flower becomes. In the same way, no matter what has been done to you, what has been spoken over you, or even the choices you may have made, this is your God-appointed season to bloom. I developed the phrase 'Blooming From The Pain Within.' A few years later, I attended Sarah Jakes' "In Real Life" (IRL) tour, where I learned about Dr. Anita Philips' book, "The Garden Within." It prompted me to realize that I was not living up to who and what God called me to be. It was time to tell my story and BLOOM!!!!! The journey will not always be easy; it will require prayer, perseverance, and pressing through trials. But take heart, Sis: Take heart, Bro: you are God's masterpiece, and with His strength, you are worth every bit of the fight. It is impossible to know who you are without knowing whose you are.

REFLECTIVE *Questions*

1. How has being treated as "the outsider", whether in your family, relationships, or community, shaped the way you see yourself and your sense of belonging? What parts of you have you hidden, silenced, or doubted because of that experience?

    ....

    ....

    ....

    ....

2. As you reflect on your journey of rediscovering identity, how might you begin to separate who you *truly are* from the painful words, actions, and labels that others placed on you? What would it look like to reclaim your worth and bloom from the pain within?

    ....

    ....

    ....

    ....

CHAPTER
Three

BROKEN SCATTERED PIECES

For I know the thoughts that I think toward you, says the Lord, thoughts of peace and not of evil, to give you a future and a hope.

JEREMIAH 29:11

God had already spoken over my life and predestined my destiny long before anyone spoke their negativity over me. I wish I had known this truth earlier. Perhaps then I would not have engaged in reckless behavior. I found myself entangled in relationships that were dysfunctional, toxic, and draining. At the time, I thought I was chasing love, but what I was really chasing was acceptance. I wanted to be seen, to be heard, to be needed, and most of all, to feel safe.

What I did not recognize back then was that every relationship, every situationship, every entanglement was costing me... me. Bit by bit, pieces of me were taken, and the others I gave away. I told myself I was confident, but the truth was I was broken. My self-esteem was shattered, though I masked it well. On the outside, I looked like I had it all together, but on the inside, my worth was tied to what others thought of me. How they saw me and how they treated me. I believed the misconception that I needed someone else to complete me.

The hole I was desperately trying to fill was not meant to be filled by any man; it was meant for God. I could not see it at the time. Instead, I kept searching in relationships for what I had longed for from a father. The absence of that love left a void I did not know how to name, so I tried to fill it with people who were never capable of giving me what I needed. I now know that I was battling: twins, abandonment, and rejection. Rejection and abandonment were the symptoms of the root cause of my behavior, which was a young girl who yearned to be loved, accepted, and told that I was special and beautiful by her father.

Good fathers matter. They shape how a daughter sees herself and how she learns to love. If I can be honest, I know that in some ways I may have been better off without my father's involvement. But that does not mean I did not ache for it. I still wish I had known the love of someone who valued me deeply, someone who poured into me and reminded me of my worth before I went searching for it in all the wrong places.

Men, I need to chat with the ladies for a minute? I'll be coming down your lane in a minute.

Professional Moment

Ladies, in my research, I found that a father's presence, especially when paired with emotional availability, consistent engagement, and secure attachment, plays a crucial role in shaping many aspects of a daughter's psychological development. These include self-esteem, body image, academic achievement, resilience against risky behaviors, and mental health (anxiety, depression). The quality of the relationship matters: Mere physical presence is not enough; what matters is how a father connects, affirms, sets boundaries, and supports. The presence, quality, and emotional engagement of a father in his daughter's life can substantially affect her psychological development, self-esteem, emotional health, and behavioral choices.

Gentlemen, I hear several men say, "It is what it is," that my father was not around. That is the furthest from the truth. A father-son relationship plays a protective role against high-risk behaviors. It has been proven that adolescents with present, engaged fathers are less likely to engage in delinquency, substance abuse, or early criminal activity. The father's role in discipline, when paired with warmth and consistency, teaches sons the importance of boundaries, accountability, and the value of consequences. Psychological studies suggest that sons often internalize rules and values more effectively when guided by a father figure, in part because they associate him with authority and identification. A father's involvement is not about perfection, but about presence and intentional engagement. The father-son bond shapes how boys learn to balance strength with empathy, independence with responsibility, and authority with humility. Psychology underscores that when fathers are consistently present, both physically and emotionally, their sons are more likely to thrive academically, socially, and emotionally.

Them Twins

From a personal standpoint, I can look back and see how the twins of rejection and abandonment took root early in my life. They did not just linger in the background; they grew, intertwining themselves into my emotions and behaviors, manifesting as anger, resentment, and bitterness. I was constantly searching for love, yet those same internal twins caused me to push people away, not only in romantic relationships but in friendships and other meaningful connections.

Professional Moment

Childhood abandonment and rejection leave wounds that often reach far beyond childhood. When a child experiences emotional, physical, or relational abandonment, whether through neglect, inconsistent caregiving, or rejection by a parent or significant figure, it disrupts their sense of safety, identity, and belonging. From a psychological standpoint, these early experiences can shape how an individual views themselves and the world around them. A child who feels unwanted or unseen often internalizes that pain as a belief: *"I am not enough."* Over time, this belief manifests as low self-esteem, people-pleasing behaviors, fear of intimacy, or emotional avoidance.

Unresolved abandonment can lead to attachment issues, where a person either clings to others out of fear of being left again or distances themselves emotionally to avoid further pain. It is not uncommon for these patterns to show up in adulthood as difficulty trusting others, emotional instability, anxiety, depression, or chronic loneliness. For many, rejection also shapes the nervous system itself; the body becomes wired for protection rather than connection. The mind constantly scans for signs of rejection or betrayal, even in safe relationships, creating cycles of self-sabotage. Healing, from a psychological lens, involves acknowledging the pain, challenging distorted beliefs, and learning to create secure internal attachments through therapy, self-compassion, and healthy community support. It is a process of retraining the mind and body to believe that safety and love are once again possible.

Abandonment by a parent is a unique form of abandonment trauma, deeply affecting a child's emotional and psychological development. The absence of parental support and nurturing during critical developmental stages can result in long-lasting fears of rejection and difficulties in forming healthy relationships later in life (Cruz et al., 2022).

From a spiritual perspective, abandonment and rejection attack the very foundation of who God created us to be, His beloved. The enemy uses these early experiences to whisper lies that contradict God's truth: *"You're unworthy, unseen, unloved."* But God's Word reveals that even when others reject us, He never abandons us.

"Though my father and mother forsake me, the Lord will receive me."

PSALM 27:10 (NIV)

Rejection can create spiritual disconnection, not because God leaves us, but because we begin to view Him through the lens of our pain. If a caregiver's love was conditional or inconsistent, we may unconsciously believe that God's love is the same. We question His goodness, His timing, and even His presence. Yet, the truth is that God specializes in healing what others have broken. Spiritually, healing from abandonment means reclaiming our identity as sons and daughters of God. It means learning to see ourselves not through the rejection of others, but through the reflection of His love. The love of God is constant, unconditional, and restorative. When we allow Him into those wounded spaces, He doesn't just comfort us; He transforms us.

"He heals the brokenhearted and binds up their wounds."

PSALM 147:3 (NIV)

Wholeness comes when we allow God to rewrite the narrative that pain once dictated. What once symbolized rejection becomes a testimony of restoration. Where there was abandonment, we now find adoption, for we are fully known and eternally loved by our Father in Heaven. When psychology and spirituality intersect, we recognize that healing is both clinical and divine. Therapy helps us understand *what happened to us*, while faith reminds us of *who we are in God*. Both are essential to restoring a fragmented soul.

Healing from childhood abandonment and rejection is not about forgetting what happened but about transforming how it lives within you. God's love provides the safe attachment your heart was always searching for. In His presence, you no longer live as the abandoned child but as the redeemed, restored, and chosen one.

It Is Ok To Have Jesus & A Therapist Too

~ AUTHOR UNKNOWN~

When Trying Feels Like Failing

I was tired of being sick and tired. Has anyone even been there? I'm just tired of doing the same thing and expecting a different result.

I decided I had had enough. I wanted to get my life right. What I was doing was not working, and deep down, I knew I needed something more, something deeper. Someone once told me, "Only God can heal the broken-hearted." I wanted to believe that, but I did not understand what it looked like in real life. You see, I did not grow up knowing God intimately. I attended Catholic school, but the rituals and traditions left a stronger impression than the presence of God Himself. Later, as a teenager, I occasionally went to church with my siblings, but to me, it felt too intense, too radical, so I joked, disengaged, and "played church."

But eventually, childhood turned into adulthood, and "playing church" turned into living broken. I became an adult woman searching for love in all the wrong places, fornicating, raising a child out of wedlock, and trying to fill emotional voids I did not yet understand. Let me share something real: Pregnancy brings a wave of emotions under the best of circumstances, but when you carry unhealed trauma, those emotions can feel overwhelming. It is as if the body remembers everything you have tried to forget. The physical changes can trigger old wounds, fears, and unresolved pain. I will speak more about this later in the book, but what I know now is that trauma doesn't disappear simply because life moves forward; it finds new ways to surface, often during our most vulnerable seasons.

Although I was hesitant to marry my child's father, a few members of the church told me that if I genuinely wanted to "get my life right," I needed to stop living in sin. So, out of guilt, pressure, and the desire to please God and others, I said *yes*. But what no one knew was that I was living with a secret, a painful reality that mirrored the life my mother once endured. I was trapped in a cycle of emotional, mental, and at times physical abuse, yet I told myself this was the price of redemption, the cost of trying to do the "right thing."

Psychologically, I now understand that I was operating from a place of survival, rather than stability. The part of me that longed to be loved believed that marriage might fix what was broken inside. Instead, it magnified the wounds I had yet to heal. His lifestyle, that "street pharmaceutical business," as we politely call it, left me physically alone and emotionally abandoned. The truth is, I felt that same loneliness even when he was home. There is a particular kind of emptiness that comes from being surrounded by people but still feeling unseen, unheard, and unloved. It is a quiet ache that whispers, *You don't belong here.* I now recognize that loneliness was not just about his absence; it was about the emotional disconnection I had learned to tolerate since childhood. My nervous system had become accustomed to chaos and inconsistency, so peace almost felt foreign.

Looking back, I can see that what I called love was really a trauma bond, the familiar pull toward what once hurt me, disguised as connection. It took years of healing, therapy, and spiritual restoration to understand that love should not cost you your peace.

Unwanted Memory

I will never forget one day, I was sitting on the couch, admiring my daughter. A single tear slid down my cheek and fell onto my shirt. As I looked at her, I realized she, too, had been born out of pain and into pain. That teardrop reminded me of giving birth to her, alone in the hospital, with no support from the man I cared for and no visit from the family member who lived just twenty minutes away. About a month later, a different family member came to visit. I thought this was God's way of mending what had been broken, a chance for reconnection and healing. But life does not always unfold the way we hope. One day, after walking for over an hour to the store just to clear my head, I came home to find my baby covered in vomit and tears, while my boyfriend and that family member were passed out. My instincts kicked in. I comforted my daughter, then confronted the scene, and all the anger, betrayal, and pain I had suppressed erupted. In the chaos, I remember hearing chilling words from that family member: *"Hit the B&#%$ Hit her again."* That night nearly cost me my freedom.

When it was all over, I sat in the stillness and realized something difficult but true: my daughter may have been conceived out of my longing to feel loved. I just wanted someone, anyone, to love me back. For a while, it was just the two of us against the world, and she became my reason to live.

I have to try. I have to make things right, not for me but for my daughter, right? I told myself I was doing the responsible thing, but truthfully, I was repeating patterns from which I had not yet healed. Red flags were everywhere, bright red, not pink, but I ignored them. That marriage, too, was emotionally destructive. It felt like the moment I said, "I do," the situation only worsened. All the negative words "nobody will ever love you, you are worthless, etc," came flooding into my mind. I am trying, but I feel like I a failing.

Am I the only one who has had moments in life when you give everything you have, your time, your energy, your prayers, and yet, it still feels like you are falling short? You tell yourself, *"I'm doing my best,"* but your best does not seem to be enough. You look around and see others moving forward, succeeding, and smiling, while you quietly hold yourself together with an invisible thread. It is a heavy feeling, the kind of invisible weight that doesn't just sit on your shoulders but sinks into your soul.

I know this space all too well. It is that middle ground between effort and exhaustion, where you have done all you can, and life still does not look the way you hoped. For years, I equated failure with not reaching the outcome I expected. If the marriage did not work, if the child struggled, if the dream took longer than I planned, I internalized that as *my* failure. I carried silent shame in spaces where I should have had grace for myself.

But here is what I have learned through both lived experience and professional understanding: when someone grows up in environments marked by rejection, inconsistency, or trauma, their inner critic becomes louder than their inner comforter. Psychologically, our brains get wired to seek approval as a form of safety. We learn that *being good enough* might keep us from being hurt, left, or overlooked again. So, when we try our best and still don't get the outcome we hoped for, it does not just feel disappointing; it feels personally invalidating. It stirs old messages like, *"You'll never get it right,"* or *"You're not worthy of good things."*

This is why self-compassion is an essential part of healing. Doing your best and still feeling like a failure does not mean you are one; it means your definition of success has been shaped by survival rather than self-worth. Sometimes, "doing your best" does not lead to visible results because the real transformation is happening inside. You may not see it yet, but every act of resilience, getting up when you want to give up, showing love when you feel empty, praying when you are unsure God is listening, is evidence of growth.

As a therapist, I have learned that emotional progress often looks like small, quiet victories: choosing not to shut down when triggered, forgiving yourself for past mistakes, or letting yourself rest without guilt. These are not failures; they are signs that your nervous system, your soul, and your sense of self are learning new rhythms of grace.

As a woman of faith, I have come to understand that God never asked me to be perfect; He asked me to be present. My best in one season may not look like my best in another, but His love remains the same. He is not measuring my worth by my productivity or performance, but by my willingness to keep showing up, even when I don't feel enough.

So, if you are in that place right now, doing your best and still feeling like a failure, take a breath. You are not behind; you are becoming. You are learning endurance, humility, and dependence on God in ways success could never teach you. Sometimes, it takes breaking before we realize we were never meant to hold it all together on our own. Healing begins the moment you stop judging your progress and start embracing your process.

As a professional and a woman of faith, I now understand that pain does not instantly disappear when you give your life to God. Salvation does not erase trauma; it invites you into a process of transformation. I thought surrendering my life to God would make everything better overnight. But I still wrestled with loneliness, abandonment, rejection, and the echoes of past abuse.

Healing, I have learned, is a journey, not a single moment. God did not remove my pain overnight; He met me in it. He began teaching me that healing is not about escaping your past, it's about allowing God to redeem it. As I continued my personal and spiritual growth, I began to understand that my pain was not meant to define me but to refine me, to teach me compassion, empathy, and faith that could not be shaken.

REFLECTIVE *Questions*

1. In what ways have rejection, abandonment, or unmet needs from your past influenced how you seek love, validation, or connection today? How might you begin to separate your worth from the wounds that shaped you?

   ....

   ....

   ....

   ....

2. When you think about the broken and scattered pieces of your story, how can you invite God to use those same fragments as part of your healing and purpose? What would it look like for you to trust that your "becoming" is just as sacred as your "breakthrough"?

   ....

   ....

   ....

   ....

CHAPTER
Four
HEALING DEMANDS
HONESTY

My heart carried questions that I did not yet dare to voice. But I often thought, who is this God? How could God love me? More importantly, where was He when I was going through the worst seasons of my life? I know I am not alone with these questions. Perhaps you, too, have whispered them in silence, or buried them deep in your heart, where they fester. They lie dormant and can cause a disconnect between you and God.

If I wanted to be whole, I had to be honest. But what did that look like? After all, I was taught how to be a performer. What I do know is that trauma has a way of reshaping not only how we experience the world, but how we experience ourselves. When pain becomes too overwhelming to process, the mind creates survival mechanisms, stories, and narratives that we tell ourselves to cope, function, and make sense of the chaos. These internal lies are not always intentional; they are often protective. We convince ourselves that we are fine when we are not. We tell ourselves that what happened didn't hurt as much as it did, or that we deserved it somehow. Over time, these small distortions become our truth, forming a false identity that helps us survive but prevents us from truly living.

Mistakes made under the influence of trauma often reinforce these self-deceptions. We make choices out of pain, choices rooted in fear, shame, or the need for control, and when those choices lead to regret, we hide behind justification or denial. Admitting the truth would mean confronting the root of our brokenness, and that can feel unbearable. So, we build walls of false confidence, perfectionism, or spiritual overcompensation, all while suppressing the inner truth that longs to be set free. Eventually, the lies we told to survive become the reality we live by. We forget who we were before the pain and begin identifying with the wounded version of ourselves.

This lack of self-honesty not only distances us from our authentic selves, but it also distorts how we see God. When we live in denial, we begin to project our wounds onto Him. If we have learned to hide our pain from people, we assume we must also hide it from God. If we've believed we are unworthy of love or forgiveness, we begin to believe God must feel the same. Trauma conditions us to expect rejection, so we brace ourselves for divine disappointment. We confuse God's holiness with human judgment, His correction with condemnation, and His silence with abandonment.

What I did not know was that God's desire is never to shame us; it is to sanctify us. He cannot heal what we continue to hide. In John 8:32, Jesus said, *"You shall know the truth, and the truth shall make you free."* Freedom begins with truth, not the version of truth we have created to survive, not "my truth" but the raw truth that exposes our pain and invites healing. To be honest with ourselves is to agree with God about what He already sees. It is to stop performing and start surrendering.

When we allow God's truth to confront our lies, we begin to see Him not through the lens of our trauma, but through the eyes of grace.

Friend, healing requires courage, the courage to face what we've buried and to trust that God can handle the parts of us we have tried to hide. It means peeling back the layers of survival and rediscovering the person God created before pain distorted the reflection. Only when we dare to be honest with ourselves can we experience the fullness of God's truth, love, and restoration. Are You ready to admit where you are and heal?

I think I Got It

I thought I had finally gotten myself together. I went through a divorce, remarried, had more children, and committed my life to God. On paper, it looked like the kind of story that should have ended with, *"and she lived happily ever after."*

But that wasn't my reality.

What I wrote about earlier in this book, the pain, the trauma, the unmet needs, began to resurface in unexpected ways. I started having vivid dreams that unsettled me. I was easily triggered. My emotions felt like old wounds that had never fully closed. Without realizing it, I began to sabotage the very marriage and family I had prayed for.

Professional Moment

Unresolved issues are like emotional landmines, hidden beneath the surface, waiting to explode when life or relationships get too close. When we fail to confront the pain of our past, it begins to leak into our present. We start to view others through the lens of our wounds, interpreting love as control, correction as rejection, and distance as abandonment. This often leads to self-sabotage; we push away what's healthy because it feels unfamiliar, and we cling to what's toxic because it feels safe. In relationships, unresolved issues can manifest as defensiveness, mistrust, or emotional withdrawal, all of which erode connection over time. The truth is, *it's not hurt people that hurt people; it's hurt people with unresolved issues that hurt people.* Healing doesn't just restore us; it protects the people connected to us. Until we face what's unresolved within, we will continue to repeat cycles of pain, mistaking survival for love and brokenness for identity.

It was in that season that I came across Jimmy Evans' book *Marriage on the Rock.* In it, he talked about *inner vows.* I refer to them as *silent vows,* the unspoken promises we make to ourselves in moments of pain or fear. These vows often become the invisible architects of our behaviors later in life.

Evans (2019) describes inner vows as *self-directed promises that can hinder growth and learning.* When I read that, it pierced something in me. I began to self-reflect and realized that I had made one of those silent vows long ago. I had said to myself, *"I will never let a man treat me the way my father treated my mother."*

At the time, that vow felt like strength. It felt like self-protection. But what it really did was harden me. From that vow grew a deep-rooted independence that bordered on isolation. There was no "flight" in my emotional vocabulary, only *fight*. I fought to be heard, fought to be in control, fought not to be hurt again. I fussed. I complained. And if I'm honest, my pet peeves had pet peeves.

I truly believed I was doing what was right to cultivate a healthy marriage and protect my family. But what I did not realize was that my need to control everything was choking the very peace I wanted to preserve. I had built an environment where everything had to be "just right," because deep down, chaos reminded me of my childhood, and I refused to relive that. In trying to prevent my children from ever being hurt, I thought I was protecting them; instead, I became the source of their tension.

Parenting through the lens of unresolved trauma often means living with a constant internal tug-of-war between what you *know* and what you *feel*. You may promise yourself you will do things differently, yet find yourself reacting the same way your parents did when stress or exhaustion sets in. That is because our brains are wired to return to what is familiar, even when it is unhealthy. As a mental health professional, I have seen how these patterns are not about a lack of love; they are about unhealed pain.

Professionally, I now understand that this is how trauma often works. It disguises itself as self-preservation, but in reality, it keeps us in bondage to fear. Unhealed trauma convinces us that control equals safety, but control often destroys intimacy. It keeps us from being vulnerable, and it robs our relationships of the softness and grace they need to thrive.

Personally, I had to learn that healing requires honesty, with myself, my husband, and children. It required me to admit that my strength had become my shield and that the walls I built to keep pain out were also keeping love out. I've learned I had to confront the parts of myself that were still longing for validation, still afraid of rejection, and still carrying the burden of being "the strong one." When I began to understand my triggers and extend compassion to my own story, I could finally extend that same grace to my children. Parenting stopped being about perfection and became about presence. The truth is that children do not need flawless parents; they need *healed* ones. Lord knows I was not healed. They need parents who can apologize, reflect, and model emotional regulation. Every time we pause before reacting, every time we choose understanding over judgment, we are rewriting the script for the next generation.

Healing the inner child within allows us to parent with more empathy and awareness. Healing meant surrendering, not just to God, but to the process of unlearning. It meant recognizing that silence was no longer protection, and that my vow had to be broken, not through willpower, but through grace.

When Negative Speech Shapes the Soul

I reached a point where I was truly sick and tired of being sick and tired. I didn't want another failed marriage, and I knew that, regardless of what my husband was or was not doing, something inside of *me* had to change. I needed to get myself together, not just for the sake of my marriage, but for the sake of my own healing. I realized that a better *me* was necessary for a better *we*.

So, I took a step that terrified me: I started therapy. Then I quit. And started again. And quit again. Healing was not linear; it was messy and uncomfortable. But eventually, I found a therapist, Faye, who helped me see myself through a new lens. She gave language to what I had been living with for years: Post-Traumatic Stress Disorder, anxiety, and the silent weight of unprocessed trauma. Through her guidance, I learned that my feelings were valid, my pain was real, and my voice mattered. For the first time in a long time, I felt heard.

Faye helped me rediscover a healthy voice, the voice that fear, shame, and rejection had buried. Slowly, I began to believe that I was somebody, that I could become something purposeful and productive. But let me be honest: that belief didn't come from external validation. My husband, my friends, or even my achievements, none of that filled the void. It didn't matter how many A's I earned in college, or that I graduated with a 3.98 GPA. It didn't matter how many people told me I was beautiful, gifted, or strong. None of it meant anything until I believed it.

The truth was that my negative self-talk was louder than every voice of encouragement around me. The echoes of my past, the unhealed words spoken over me as a child, were still shaping how I saw myself. My inner child was still wounded by those who should have spoken life into me, but instead spoke destruction and death. Those words became my internal soundtrack, and yes, words hurt, and they stick.

As an adult, I realized that every time I spoke harshly to myself, I was reopening old wounds, pulling the scab off what God was trying to heal. When I looked in the mirror, I didn't see who I was becoming; I only saw what *they said*. It took time, faith, and consistent inner work to quiet those voices and replace them with truth: *I am who God says I am. I am not my past, my pain, or their words.*

Words have power. They can breathe life or slowly steal it. When a child grows up under the sound of harsh words, words that cut instead of comfort, criticize instead of correct, or shame instead of shape, it creates wounds that the eye cannot see but the heart cannot forget. As children, we naturally look to those around us to understand who we are. The words spoken over us become mirrors, reflecting back an image we learn to believe. When my parents or siblings said, *"You'll never amount to anything,"* my child's mind absorbed it as truth. When they constantly compared or belittled me, my young heart learned, *"I'm not enough."* Over time, these words begin to echo in the subconscious. Just like they did to me, some of you can attest to the same thing. These words shape our thoughts, behaviors, and relationships long after childhood comes to an end.

Professional Moment

Negative speech impacts a child's developing sense of self. The brain records emotional memories more vividly than neutral ones, so painful words imprint deeply. Children who grow up in environments of criticism often internalize those voices, carrying them into adulthood as an inner dialogue. That once external criticism becomes internal condemnation. Instead of needing someone else to tell them they are unworthy, they start doing it themselves.

"It is estimated that during the first 18 years of life, if you grew up in a reasonably positive home, as much as 77% of the programming you received was negative. The good news is that replacing negative programs often takes weeks, not years." Shad Helmstetter, PH.D.

As adults, we may struggle with confidence, boundaries, or trust. They might overwork, overgive, or overperform, trying to prove we are worthy of love. Did I mention this is how individuals become people pleasers? Others withdraw completely, afraid that if they ever let people close, the words of rejection will return. Even when God calls them *chosen, loved, and enough,* their inner critic argues otherwise, reminding them of every insult they've ever absorbed.

Spiritually, negative words plant lies that compete with God's truth. Scripture tells us, "Death and life are in the power of the tongue" (Proverbs 18:21). Words can either align with heaven's identity or partner with the enemy's deception. When children hear constant negativity, it distorts their ability to hear God's voice clearly. But here's the good news: what was spoken *over* you does not have to define what's spoken *through* you. God can rewrite every false narrative with His truth.

REFLECTIVE *Questions*

1. What protective stories or "inner vows" have you told yourself to survive pain, and how might those narratives still be shaping how you love, trust, or respond to God and others today?

    ....

    ....

    ....

    ....

2. In what areas of your life have you been performing strength instead of practicing honesty? What might begin to change if you allowed God's truth to meet you in the very places you've been hiding?

    ....

    ....

    ....

    ....

CHAPTER
Five

REDEEMED FROM
THE FRAGMENTS

Whole. I heard it said, I heard people talk about it, but what is whole? How do you become whole? On my quest to find answers that would allow me to walk in the reason I was created, because surely, I was not created for other people's sick pleasures or for my unhealthy decision-making, I finally surrendered and sought God for answers men could not give. Now that I was honest with myself, I needed to know, according to Him, who I am, what my purpose is, how He sees me, and why I was created.

It was in this season that I finally understood something life-changing: that I am a trichotomy: spirit, soul, and body. Every part of me is connected, and when one part hurts, the others feel it too. Seeing myself through God's eyes helped me realize that my healing couldn't just be surface level; it had to reach the deepest parts of who I am. My trauma did not just wound my emotions; it broke my spirit, tarnished my body, and tried to claim my soul. I needed healing in every part of me, and only God could put me back together again.

The Trichotomy of Man

- **Spirit** – (Gets regenerated through Christ) Our spirit has been given so the soul can express itself spiritually and connect with God. The soul and the spirit are housed in our body/flesh.

  The spirit is intended to have dominion, to rule over the natural/carnal man.

  In scripture, carnality refers to everything in man that is not under the control of the holy spirit.

- **Soul** – (Eternal) Let me say this: a person does not have a soul; we are a living soul. **Genesis 2:7** And the Lord God formed man *of* the dust of the ground, and breathed into his nostrils the breath of life; and man became a living being. Our soul comes from God; it is the core of who we are and gives life to the body.

  A healthy soul is a submitted will, intellect, and emotional being

  The dysfunctional soul is carnal and lacks control.

- **Body** – (Temporary) The soul is what animates it; without the soul, the body is just a shell. The body has been given to humans so that the soul can express itself physically.

  These are not opposite terms but rather terms that supplement one another to describe aspects of the inseparable whole person.

Now may the God of peace Himself sanctify[a] you completely; and may your whole spirit, soul, and body be preserved blameless at the coming of our Lord Jesus Christ.

1 THESSALONIANS 5:23

This scripture reminds us that God's sanctification is not limited to behavior; it reaches every dimension of who we are. Healing, growth, and holiness are not compartmentalized. God does not just save our spirit and leave our emotions broken or our bodies enslaved by unhealthy habits. He desires complete restoration, a healed soul, a renewed mind, a pure heart, and a body that glorifies Him.

We are uniquely crafted by God. Out of all creations, only humans carry this ability to reason, to choose, and to plan. Animals live by instinct, but we were made in the image of God. That image is carried in our soul. There are no two souls alike. Your soul is uniquely yours, your laughter, your tears, your preferences, your personality. Ezekiel 18:4 declares, *"All souls are Mine."* Whether saved or unsaved, every soul belongs to God and will return to Him for judgment. This means our souls were created not only to animate our bodies, but to connect us to the eternal. Our souls stand at the intersection of the physical and the spiritual, bridging the seen and unseen.

Determined to continue walking in honesty, I had to tell myself that, although I understood what these scriptures meant, my first thought was, *Wait a minute, can I be made whole when I've been broken for so long?* Can God really do that for me? Will He do it for me? Yes, I had those questions, even as a Christian. Spirit-filled, tongue-talking, foot-stomping, hand-clapping, you know the type. Yet despite giving my life to Christ and building what I thought was a strong relationship with Him, I still carried unresolved wounds that distorted my perception of who God truly was. I realized I had placed God inside a man's box, limiting Him to the measure of my pain and experiences. My lens was cracked, and I was trying to see a perfect God through the shattered pieces of my past.

Lord, help my dysfunctional thoughts. Can I tell you I was scared? I have been functioning in dysfunction so long that it felt normal. What does being whole look and feel like?

Friend, this is what I learned. Your soul matters deeply to God. It is His breath within you. It is the eternal core of who you are. And it is the place He longs to heal, restore, and align with His will.

The truth is, God never abandoned me, and He has never abandoned you. Scripture reminds us in Deuteronomy 31:6, *"For the Lord your God goes with you; He will never leave you nor forsake you."* But when your soul is broken, it can be hard to believe that. Pain clouds our vision, and trauma convinces us that God must have turned away. Yet God is not afraid of our questions. In fact, He invites us to bring them to Him.

In Psalm 42:5, David cries out, *"Why, my soul, are you downcast? Why so disturbed within me? Put your hope in God, for I will yet praise Him, my Savior and my God."* Even David, a man after God's own heart, wrestled with a downcast soul. But he learned to speak hope into his own spirit and remind himself of God's presence.

If you feel broken or incomplete, know this: you are not meant to stay that way. Wholeness is possible. Healing is possible. Redemption is possible because Christ has already made a way. You are a spirit. You are a soul. You are a body. But most importantly, you are God's beloved creation, designed to live whole in Him.

Friend, I hear you. But how?

From Wounded to Whole

Let me address "Whole" from both a psychological and spiritual perspective.

To be *whole* means to live in a state of internal harmony, self-acceptance, and integration. It reflects the process of aligning the various parts of oneself, the mind, emotions, and behaviors, so that they work together rather than against each other.

A whole person acknowledges every part of their story, the pain, the joy, the wounds, and the triumphs, without denial or fragmentation. It means no longer rejecting or suppressing parts of yourself that feel broken or unworthy but learning to embrace and integrate them into a unified sense of self.

Psychologically, wholeness is often linked with concepts such as:

- **Self-awareness:** understanding your thoughts, feelings, and motivations.

- **Emotional regulation:** managing emotions healthily and adaptively.

- **Authenticity:** living in alignment with your true values and identity.

- **Healing from trauma:** processing past wounds so they no longer dictate present behavior.

- **Resilience and growth:** developing the capacity to learn and evolve through life's challenges.

In essence, wholeness in psychology is not perfection; it is integration. It is freedom to be your *entire self* without shame or fragmentation.

From a spiritual and biblical perspective, *wholeness* means to be complete, restored, and at peace in your relationship with God, yourself, and others. The Hebrew word often translated as "peace", Shalom, carries this meaning of *wholeness, completeness, and well-being.*

In Scripture, God's desire has always been for His people to live whole, not just physically, but spiritually, emotionally, and relationally. Wholeness is the opposite of brokenness caused by sin, trauma, or separation from God. It is being brought back into divine alignment through Christ, who came to restore what was lost.

- **Wholeness is restoration:** "He restores my soul" (Psalm 23:3).

- **Wholeness is peace:** "You will keep in perfect peace those whose minds are steadfast, because they trust in You" (Isaiah 26:3).

- **Wholeness is healing:** "Daughter, your faith has made you whole" (Mark 5:34 KJV).

- **Wholeness is living in purpose:** "Beloved, I pray that you may prosper in all things and be in health, just as your soul prospers" (3 John 1:2).

Spiritually, being whole means living from a healed and surrendered soul, a place where your heart, mind, and spirit are aligned with God's truth and love. It is not the absence of pain but the presence of divine peace and purpose amid life's imperfections.

That is why so many of us wrestle with unexplainable emptiness. No matter how much we accomplish, with whom we are, or what we achieve, something still feels missing. We chase success, love, and validation, yet the void remains. That is because this space was never meant for people or possessions; it was designed for God. He alone can occupy the deepest part of our soul. From a psychological perspective, we often try to soothe this emptiness through distraction or attachment, but true peace cannot be manufactured; it must be received. From a spiritual perspective, this longing is divine; it is the soul's reminder that we were created for communion with our Creator.

We are not truly whole until our spirit reconnects with His presence. To be whole is to be *healed, aligned, and authentic,* to live from a place where your internal world reflects peace, acceptance, and divine connection.

- **Psychologically,** wholeness is the integration of the self.

- **Spiritually,** wholeness is reconciliation with God and restoration of the soul.

Wholeness is not something we achieve once and for all; it is a lifelong process of healing, growing, and walking in truth, becoming who God originally designed us to be: emotionally balanced, spiritually anchored, and fully alive.

REFLECTIVE *Questions*

1. In what areas of your life do you still feel fragmented or disconnected, spiritually, emotionally, or physically, and what would it look like to invite God into those places to begin restoring wholeness?

   ....

   ....

   ....

   ....

2. How have your past wounds or distorted views of God shaped the way you see yourself today? What truths about who God says you are can begin to replace the lies that pain once told to you?

   ....

   ....

   ....

   ....

CHAPTER
Six

WHEN
ATTACHMENTS
SHAPE YOUR SOUL

Through prayer, reflection, and conversations with people from all walks of life, I came to understand that wholeness requires more than just being honest with myself. Honesty was the beginning, but healing demanded more. I had already traced the root of my patterns, the seed that fed my behaviors, my choices, and my emotional and mental unrest. But now I had to confront what had grown from it. I had to do the hard work: uproot what no longer served me, cut ties, both the ones I recognized and the ones buried beneath the surface.

There was a time in my life when I didn't understand why I loved the way I did, why I clung so tightly to people who were no good for me, or why I pushed away those who genuinely cared. I had to understand why I kept choosing, and even attracting, certain types of relationships, companions, and friends who reflected wounds I hadn't fully addressed.

I'll never forget it, the cycle that looked like love. I was nineteen and thought I was in a relationship with, let me call him "Dyllian". Later, I realized it was a situationship. Even after I found out he had cheated, I stayed. There were apologies, gifts, trips, and empty bandages over a broken heart. But then came the late nights, the unexplained disappearances, the arguing. Days would pass without seeing him.

When I could not be around him, I clung to his family just to feel close, something, anything. His cousins reassured me he loved me. "He just needs space," they said. But his aunt pulled me aside and told me the truth: "I know my nephew. He is no good." I did not listen. Why would I? He was still giving me what I thought was love.

Then came the call. There were no cell phones back then; just house phones. A woman's voice told me she had been dating him, too. She described his house down to the details. We planned to catch him together, and we did. Words flew, emotions erupted. You'd think that would be the end. But it was not.

The cycle restarted: gifts, sweet talk, trips. His family stood by me, claiming they would not allow any other woman to be around me. I believed them. I wanted to. A few months later, I ran into the other woman again. Heated words and threats; it felt final. But it was not.

One evening, I saw a familiar truck pull up. "Dyllian" was inside. His cousins, those same ones who told me they loved me, got out and tried to jump me. They failed, thanks to some neighbors who stepped in. Later, I learned the woman was pregnant with twins. His twins.

I was devastated. But even then, I let him explain. I listened. I said my peace. And like anyone stuck in an unhealthy pattern, I did not heal; I just moved on to the next relationship, carrying the same wounded soul. I did not realize it at the time, but I was not chasing love. I was chasing validation, masking deep insecurities and calling it love.

That cycle did not start with "Dyllian", and it did not end with him either. I now know that what looked like love was really fear in disguise, fear of being alone, fear of not being enough, fear that maybe this was all I deserved. My behavior was not irrational; it was protective. I clung to dysfunction because it felt familiar. Safe, even.

As a therapist, I've come to realize that many of the behaviors we label as *problems* are actually patterns of protection. They are survival responses, learned ways of attaching that began long before we had the words to explain them. And as a woman who has walked through trauma, disappointment, and rejection, I've lived the reality of how those attachments can feel like chains around the soul.

Friend, it is essential to understand your attachment style, as it provides insight into how you love, relate, and heal. Why you think, feel, and behave the way you do, and how those behaviors influence the quality and stability of your relationships.

When Protection Looks Like a Problem

From both personal experience and professional observation, as I mentioned previously in this chapter, I have learned that many behaviors we label as "problematic" are actually patterns of protection, strategies that the mind and body adopt to keep us safe when safety feels out of reach. What looks like dysfunction is often a survival strategy, an unconscious attempt to shield ourselves from emotional harm. These behaviors are not random; they're learned, rehearsed, and reinforced through lived experience. And over time, they shape how we connect, or fail to connect, with others. At one point in my life, I used to think my need to be in control, my fear of vulnerability, or my emotional withdrawal were flaws to fix. But looking deeper, I realized they were armor, built to protect a younger version of me who did not feel safe trusting others. I was defending myself from abandonment, rejection, or disappointment before it could happen. These weren't just personality quirks; they were attachment injuries in disguise. Does any of this sound familiar?

Professional Moment

I see the same patterns play out in clients. Behaviors like emotional avoidance, clinginess, people-pleasing, hyper-independence, or explosive reactions are often misread as immaturity, stubbornness, or dysfunction. But through a trauma-informed lens, they make perfect sense. As Dr. Bessel van der Kolk explains in *The Body Keeps the Score* (2014), the nervous system learns to expect danger where it once existed, and acts accordingly, even when that danger is no longer present.

A person who pushes people away at the slightest sign of closeness is not being "difficult"; they are protecting themselves. These protective patterns directly contribute to dysfunctional attachment styles. For example, someone with an anxious attachment style may cling or overfunction in relationships, driven by a fear of abandonment. This is not neediness; it's an attempt to stay emotionally safe. On the flip side, avoidant attachment often stems from a belief that intimacy leads to pain. So the person withdraws, keeps emotional distance, or numbs out, not because they don't care, but because closeness feels threatening. As Bowlby's attachment theory suggests, early interactions with caregivers shape our internal working models of relationships (Bowlby, 1988). If care was inconsistent, neglectful, or chaotic, we internalize that as the blueprint for future connection.

Someone who cannot sit still or focus is not necessarily defiant or lazy; they may be operating from a dysregulated nervous system that never learned how to feel safe. Even procrastination, often viewed as laziness, can be a way to avoid shame or fear tied to performance, failure, or judgment (Pychyl & Sirois, 2016). What society often views as "toxic" behavior is, at its root, a trauma-informed adaptation. When we understand that, we can meet ourselves and others with more compassion and less judgment. This does not excuse the harm that these patterns can cause, but it does provide a starting point for healing. By identifying the protective purpose behind the pattern, we can begin to unlearn it and build safer, more secure attachments.

Healing began when I stopped asking why they treated me that way and started asking why I accepted it. *What was this behavior trying to protect me from?* The answer usually leads us straight to the wound, and eventually, to the repair.

My answer was painful: I was emotionally attached to a version of myself that believed love was supposed to hurt, that endurance equaled loyalty, and that leaving meant failure. None of that was true.

It took years to unlearn. It took prayer, therapy, self-reflection, and grace. But eventually, I began to see the difference between love and attachment, between security and control, between consistency and manipulation. I started choosing differently, and more importantly, I started seeing myself differently.

Because healing doesn't start with others changing, it starts when we choose to.

Where Attachment Begins

Our first human attachment forms with our mother or primary caregiver. That bond becomes the blueprint for how we connect to others, and even how we connect to God.

We each carry into adulthood the blueprint of how connections were formed in early life, how our caregivers responded to our needs, how safe we felt to reach out, and how reliable their returns really were. According to attachment theory, first articulated by John Bowlby and advanced by Mary Ainsworth, these early connections form an internal working model of self and others that remains active in our adult relationships.

Professional Moment

When we become aware of *which* attachment style we carry, we begin to see not only *why* we behave the way we do in relationships, but also *how* our behavior shapes the life of the soul. A good book to assist you in identifying your attachment style and overcoming it is "*The Attachment Theory Workbook: Powerful Tools to Promote Understanding, Increase Stability & Build Lasting Relationships*. By Annie Chen. For now, here are the four core styles and how they tend to manifest in the dance of connection.

1. **Secure Attachment**

   In this style, the person learned that reaching out was safe, that comfort was available, and that they themselves were worthy of care. In adult relationships, secure-attached individuals tend to:

   - Feel comfortable being close to others and also being independent.

   - Communicate their feelings, seek support, and provide it without losing themselves.

   - Navigate conflict with resilience and self-regulation rather than retreat or attack.

   For the soul, secure attachment means being known and valued; the "ties" are safe, nourishing, and freeing rather than binding. This foundation often enables healthier patterns, deeper trust, and greater relational freedom.

2. **Anxious (Ambivalent) Attachment**

   This style arises when early care was inconsistent, sometimes responsive, sometimes absent or unpredictable. In adulthood, those with anxious attachment may:

   - Crave closeness but fear abandonment; question their partner's love or presence.

   - Become hyper-vigilant to relational cues, prone to cling, worry, or emotional reactivity.

   - Shape relationships by leaning in desperately, hoping intimacy will quiet the fear, yet often triggering the very distance they dread.

   For the soul, this ties the heart to the rhythm of "If I must hold on, maybe they'll stay." The relational scaffolding is shaky, and the longing remains unquiet. Healing the soul means learning that love and connection can rest on safety, not just urgency.

3. **Avoidant (Dismissive) Attachment**

   When a child learns that reaching out is met with indifference, rejection, or shame, the coping strategy may become *I'll do it myself.* In adult life:

   - The avoidant person values independence so highly that they may resist intimacy, emotional vulnerability, or dependence.

- They may minimize feelings, distance themselves when things get "too real," and interpret closeness as a threat.

- Their relationships may seem fine on the surface, but are marked by emotional undercurrent: solitude disguised as strength.

For the soul, the wound is often: *I don't need you; I can handle it alone.* Yet underneath this posture lies a quiet ache for connection. Healing the soul means discovering that strength doesn't mean solitude, and intimacy need not be dangerous.

4. **Disorganized (Fearful-Avoidant) Attachment**

This style often emerges in childhood when the caregiver was both loved and feared, perhaps due to trauma, neglect, or chaos. Adults with disorganized attachment may:

- Crave closeness and yet fear it simultaneously; feel torn between approach and avoidance.

- Show unpredictable relational patterns: sometimes clingy, sometimes detached.

- Bear relational trauma in their souls, carrying the story of "I want connection, but I'm afraid of it." For the soul, the ties are tangled: yearning and fear in the same breath. Healing means unwinding the confusion, embracing safety, and trusting that closeness need not bring harm.

Our attachment style is not just a psychological label; it is a soul posture toward connection. Developmental psychologist Erik Erikson taught that our first stage of life is *trust versus mistrust*. When our needs for safety, comfort, and affection are met, we learn to trust. When they're not, mistrust takes root, and our hearts begin to protect themselves. Fast forward to adulthood, and those early roots bear fruit in our relationships. We chase love that mirrors our chaos. We avoid intimacy because it feels unsafe. We try to fix others so we can avoid facing our own wounds. The truth is, our childhood environment and family dynamics have built emotional reflexes, many of which were formed in response to survival, not safety.

But what if I told you that your first connection was with God? When I understood this, it changed my life. My *first attachment* was not to my mother or my circumstances; it was to God. Before anyone ever spoke over me, He knew me, He put destiny in me, He breathed life into me.

"For You created my inmost being; You knit me together in my mother's womb."

PSALM 139:13–14 (NIV)

That word *knit* means deliberate, careful, intentional. God paid attention to every detail of your design. He was not careless. He was *creative*.

And Jeremiah 1:5 takes it further: "

Before I formed you in the womb, I knew you."

Whether your parents had a plan or not, God had a purpose for you. You were not a mistake. Regardless of how you were conceived, Romans 8:28 says *And we know that for those who love God all things work together for good, for those who are called according to his purpose NIV*. That means before your first cry, He had already spoken destiny into your spirit. We were first *spiritually connected* to God, our soul remembers. That is why that longing you feel, that emptiness you cannot fill, those relationships you chase, it is your soul crying out to reconnect with the One who first called you *His own*.

We are bound to all of this because sin entered the world and distorted that original connection. I am not saying you are a bad person; I am saying you are a human being living in a fallen world. Every weakness, deficiency, and inadequacy traces back to the moment humanity disconnected from God's divine order. That is why we listen to so many other voices, our flesh, our fears, our pain, until God's voice becomes faint. Paul said in Romans 7:21-25, *"When I want to do good, evil is right there with me."* Even those who love God can struggle with habits, temptations, and cycles they cannot seem to break. The enemy knows this, which is why he whispers lies that sound like the truth. He tempts your flesh to influence your soul, just like he did with Eve. And the more we attach ourselves to things outside of God, whether it is toxic relationships, emotional dependencies, sexual soul ties (I will talk more about this in the upcoming chapters), or the things we feed our minds through music, media, or conversation, the more disconnected we become from who He created us to be.

We must understand that whatever we attach ourselves to other than God has the power to pull us away from Him. But the good news is this: what has been disconnected can be restored. God designed the brain and the soul to *heal*. Dr. Helmstetter calls it "rewriting the mind," but Scripture calls it *renewing the mind*.

Romans 12:2 reminds us, *"Be transformed by the renewing of your mind."*

So, what does that mean for you, friend? It means your healing begins with reconnection, reconnecting to God's truth, to your divine identity, and to the voice that first called you whole. You do not have to live bound by attachments or haunted by the past. You can reprogram the negativity, redownload your identity, and rediscover your worth in Christ.

Because before the world ever named you broken, God called you *healed*.

REFLECTIVE *Questions*

1. What relationships, habits, or emotional attachments have you held onto that may have once felt like protection but are now preventing your soul from healing and growing? How might releasing them create space for divine connection and peace?

    ....

    ....

    ....

    ....

2. In what ways have your early experiences of love, rejection, or inconsistency shaped the way you attach to others, and even to God? What would it look like to begin forming secure, faith-centered attachments that align with how He originally designed you to connect?

    ....

    ....

    ....

    ....

CHAPTER
Seven
THE COST OF BELONGING

M y mother used to say, "Show me your company and I will tell you your name." As a kid, it did not mean much. It sounded like one of those sayings parents toss around to keep you out of trouble. But as I became emotionally and mentally whole, I understood exactly what she meant. The people we connect with, the crowds we roll with, and the relationships we build have the power to shape who we become, our values, our choices, and our identity.

From a professional lens, this need to belong is rooted in human psychology. Maslow named it a basic need: love and belonging. When we do not receive affirmation from healthy places, we often seek it in unhealthy ones. And the soul, when wounded, does not care if the bond is toxic, as long as it feels like a connection.

Personally, I have lived this truth. I used to hang out with a crew that did not reflect who I was at my core. They smoked weed and cigarettes, drank heavily, sold drugs, everything that shouted, "the streets." I was not into smoking or drinking, and they respected that. But I still carried guns. I was known as "the one not to mess with." I never sold drugs, but I hid them. I was present when deals went down. So yes, I was involved. I was just as much a part of the world I knew I was not built for.

Why? Because being around them gave me clout. And more than that, they made me feel like I belonged, like I was wanted, and like I was seen. That is what I really craved, not the lifestyle, but the sense of family. It did not matter that it went against what I knew deep down was right. I stayed because they treated me like I mattered. And when you do not feel that anywhere else, it is easy to trade your peace for a place at the enemy's table.

Looking back, I see how that desire to belong led me into bonds that were more about survival than love. More about identity than integrity. I wrapped myself in false loyalty to avoid facing my own loneliness. And what I thought was strength, being fearless, being hard, being loyal to the streets, was just a disguise for pain. Maybe this is not your story, but many of us can relate to seeking connections, forming friendships, entering relationships, or even joining social circles, not out of genuine alignment, but simply to belong, to feel seen, or to avoid being alone.

Professionally, I now understand that these kinds of attachments are often trauma-based. They grow out of early wounds, neglect, abandonment, and rejection, leaving us looking for validation wherever we can find it. And until we recognize that, we repeat the cycle: unhealthy people, unhealthy places, unhealthy love.

Healing meant unlearning the lie that I had to become something I was not to be accepted. It meant grieving the false sense of family I once had and building a real connection with people who valued me without conditions. It meant honoring the girl in me, who only wanted to be loved, while protecting the woman I was becoming. Because not all belongings are healthy. And not every bond deserves to survive the healing. I was losing my soul. The healed soul learns to choose differently, not from fear of rejection, but from a place of self-respect. And that is the kind of belonging that does not cost your peace or your purpose.

Bound by Design

This healing journey assisted me in understanding just how removed from God I was. Now, when I think about soul ties, I do not see them as accidents or coincidences; they were part of God's original design. However, being separated from God, I learned that they were not Godly relationships and that was not God's design for them. From the very beginning, humanity was created for connection: spirit to Spirit, and soul to soul. We were never meant to live disconnected. The very essence of who we are was never meant to exist in isolation. We were created to attach, to bond, and to be in relationship. The soul tie, at its purest form, was God's divine idea of spiritual and emotional connection, not a curse, but a covenantal bond that mirrors His desire for intimacy with us.

God had a divine intention in connection with us. When God breathed life into Adam, He did more than give him existence; He gave him communion. Genesis 2:7 says, *"And the Lord God formed man of the dust of the ground and breathed into his nostrils the breath of life; and man became a living soul."*

(NKJV). That breath was not just oxygen; it was union. It was the first soul tie, a sacred connection between Creator and creation.

Before Eve ever entered the picture, Adam was tied to God. Before there was sin, before there was shame, there was fellowship. God and Adam shared an exclusive relationship, one built on trust, intimacy, and spiritual connection. This divine connection became the blueprint for every other relationship that would follow. Adam did not have to strive for God's presence; it was natural. Their time together was not a duty; it was a rhythm. They were connected spirit to Spirit. The problem arises when we become more bonded to people, pain, or past experiences than to the One who gave us life.

I often compare this to a baby in the womb. The umbilical cord is the lifeline; the baby receives oxygen, nourishment, and sustenance from its mother. If that cord is cut too soon, the baby cannot survive. That's how vital our spiritual connection with God is. He is our source of life.

When God said to Jeremiah, *"Before I formed you in your mother's womb, I knew you"* (Jeremiah 1:5), He was revealing something sacred, that before we ever connected to our earthly source, we were already connected to our divine one. Our relationship with God isn't accidental or conditional; it's inherent. We are sustained, nurtured, and given identity through that connection. Even after the fall, God never stopped desiring a relationship with His people. In Leviticus 26:12, He said, *"I will walk among you and be your God, and you shall be My people"* (NKJV). That was His way of saying, "Even though you have fallen, my desire for connection remains."

From a psychological perspective, attachment is essential for survival. Healthy attachment provides security, validation, and belonging. It tells the soul, *"You are safe to love and to be loved."* But when attachment is inconsistent, neglectful, or abusive, it creates wounds that distort how we perceive connection. The same God-given need for attachment becomes the very area where brokenness manifests. That is why the soul tie, originally designed for good, can either nurture or entangle the heart, depending on who and what we are bonded with.

When we are spiritually connected to God, His nature flows through us. Every other relationship flows from that secure foundation. We love better because we are loved perfectly. We forgive each other because we have been forgiven. We attach without fear because perfect love has cast it out (1 John 4:18).

God's Blueprint for Soul Connection

A healthy soul-to-soul connection allows a two-way flow of love, empathy, and growth. When we connect with others through shared values, emotional honesty, and mutual care, our souls thrive. These bonds can be life-giving when aligned with God's design, relationships that nurture, not drain; build, not break; heal, not harm.

Professional Moment

As a counselor, I have learned that many of our emotional struggles come from misaligned attachments, bonds formed through unmet needs, trauma, or fear. Yet even that reveals something important: we are *wired* for attachment. It is how God made us. The same need that drives us to form relationships also invites us to evaluate what (and who) we are tied to. We know that attachment begins before birth. A mother provides not only physical nourishment but also emotional and genetic influence. Through her, a child receives DNA, personality traits, and even predispositions. These early patterns affect how we think, feel, and relate as adults.

Some inherit stability, warmth, and empathy; others inherit anxiety, emotional volatility, or even patterns of addiction. These inherited tendencies shape how we bond, whether we cling, avoid, or connect securely. Understanding this helps us show compassion to ourselves. We cannot heal what we do not understand, and we cannot release what we will not name.

Spiritual Purpose

Spiritually, soul ties reflect covenant. Every time we join ourselves emotionally, physically, or spiritually with another person, a bond is formed. 1 Corinthians 6:17 reminds us, *"But he who is joined to the Lord becomes one spirit with Him."* God's design was that our deepest bond would always be with Him. Yet when our soul becomes tied to what was never meant to hold us, toxic relationships, unresolved trauma, and unhealthy dependence, our spiritual and emotional balance becomes disrupted. The tie that once served a purpose now becomes a prison. Healing, then, begins with untangling what was never ordained and restoring that bond to divine alignment.

Healing the Misaligned Tie

This begins by recognizing that unhealthy soul ties are not about shame; it is about reclaiming the sacredness of your soul's design. God wants to heal the parts of you still tied to pain, rejection, or the need for validation. Philippians 1:6 declares, *"He who began a good work in you will carry it on to completion until the day of Christ Jesus."* Friend, healing happens when you invite God to become your primary attachment, when your emotional security is anchored in His love rather than human approval. Therapy, prayer, and self-awareness all become tools of grace, working together to restore what was broken. Our *spirit* connects to God. Our *soul* connects to others. Our *body* connects us to the world around us.

Our bodies are the vessels through which the soul experiences and interacts with the world. They carry the imprints of our stories, our joys, traumas, and transformations. When assisting my clients in healing from trauma, I describe the body as the bridge between the physical and the spiritual. It receives, stores, and expresses what our souls have endured. Research in the field of psychophysiology shows that the body holds emotional memory; unresolved trauma can manifest through chronic pain, tension, and illness (van der Kolk, 2014). This is why

Scripture reminds us in *1 Corinthians 6:19 that our bodies are temples of the Holy Spirit,* sacred spaces designed not only for function but for fellowship with God. When we move, breathe, touch, and engage in the world, we are participating in both a physical and spiritual exchange. Healing, therefore, is holistic. As the mind renews and the soul restores, the body responds; it releases what it once carried in silence and learns to live in harmony with the peace of God.

REFLECTIVE *Questions*

1. In what ways have you compromised your peace, purpose, or identity just to feel accepted or connected? What would it look like to belong without losing yourself, to choose relationships that affirm your worth rather than require you to prove it?

   ....

   ....

   ....

   ....

2. How have your past attachments, whether to people, pain, or patterns, shaped your understanding of connection and belonging? How can you begin to realign your attachments to reflect God's original design for a divine and healthy relationship?

   ....

   ....

   ....

   ....

CHAPTER
Eight

FROM CONNECTION
TO ENTANGLEMENT

I'll never forget the day a minister looked at me and said, "Most of your spiritual turmoil is connected to ungodly soul ties." I know what you're thinking: how did we even get to that kind of conversation? Well, friend, the truth is that certain behaviors were showing up in my relationship that did not belong there. They were not born out of that relationship; they were remnants of my past, unhealed wounds still speaking through my actions. Deep down, I did not just want to be healed; I wanted to be whole. I wanted freedom that would allow me to love and be loved in a healthy way. That conversation stirred something in me; it was not enough to just hear it; I needed to *understand* it. What is a soul tie? So, I sought wisdom, therapy, and spiritual guidance to uncover what was really happening within me. We will unpack those behaviors together throughout this chapter. But for now, in my nephew Tommy's voice from The Steve Harvey Morning Show, *"Buckle up and hold on for the ride."*

Understanding Soul Ties

But before we explore what a soul-tie truly is, I want to remind you of a foundational truth: your soul is more than just a poetic idea. It is your inner being, your emotions, thoughts, personality, and your will. It is where your heart lives, and yes, your soul keeps receipts. Every experience, every relationship, every wound, it records them all.

From a spiritual perspective, the soul is where deep bonds form, intentionally or unintentionally. And while God designed soul connections to serve a purpose, such as unity, intimacy, and covenant, the enemy is always looking to pervert what God created. Where there is divine design, there is often demonic distortion.

Professional Moment

As a Minister, licensed counselor, certified life coach, and disciple of Christ, I have seen the impact of soul-ties firsthand. People walk into my office bound by relationships that no longer serve them, weighed down by emotional habits, toxic attachments, and mental and spiritual confusion. These ties can manifest as anxiety, depression, people-pleasing, addictive behaviors, and relational dysfunction. They don't just affect how a person feels; they shape who a person becomes.

Are Soul-Ties Biblical?

The term *"soul-tie"* does not appear directly in Scripture, but the concept certainly does. The Bible gives us insight into the nature of soul connections, both healthy and unhealthy.

Take *2 Corinthians 6:14, for example: "Do not be unequally yoked together with unbelievers. For what fellowship has righteousness with lawlessness? And what communion has light with darkness?" (NKJV).* Now, I know some people believe this verse only applies to marriage, but the Bible never limits it that way. Yoking is about alignment, about connection. When you are yoked with someone, mentally, emotionally, or spiritually, you move together. Their pace affects your pace. Their direction affects your direction. That is why it is so dangerous to be yoked to someone you are not spiritually aligned with.

Another example is found in 1 Samuel 18:1: *"Now when he had finished speaking to Saul, the soul of Jonathan was knit to the soul of David, and Jonathan loved him as his own soul" (NKJV).* This is a soul-tie in its purest form, godly, loyal, selfless. Their souls were *knit together*, a deep emotional and spiritual bond that transcended status or circumstance.

What Is a Soul-Tie?

A soul-tie is a deep connection formed through the mind, emotions, and will. It can be forged in any type of relationship:

- Familiar (family)

- Platonic (friendship)

- Romantic (intimate)

From a psychological standpoint, a soul-tie is a powerful emotional attachment, often so intense that it compromises a person's autonomy. It can feel like mind control, or a mind-link. People find themselves questioning their judgment, second-guessing their values, or staying in harmful relationships simply because they feel bound.

Soul-ties can lead to:

- Emotional dependency

- Sexual and emotional confusion

- A sense of obligation that overrides logic

- Compromised influence and decision-making

- Longing for unhealthy connections

- Difficulty detaching, even when there is no peace

Bound by Brokenness

As I look back over my life, I can now see myself in several of these examples I have been writing and teaching about. For a long time, I did not even realize that one of my relationships was both emotionally and physically abusive. In my mind, I thought, *"This can't be domestic violence, I fight back. He's called the police on me, too."*

Do not judge me, friend. That was my *unhealed self*-talking, the version of me that confused dysfunction for strength. I told myself I was trying to break the cycle in my family. Everyone around me was either divorced or in unhealthy relationships, and I refused to be another statistic. But even with all that determination, I still had trouble letting go. My peace was being stolen, yet my heart clung to the illusion of connection. As delusional as it sounds, I was emotionally dependent. In my brokenness, I thought *some* attention was better than none. I thought *somebody* caring, even if it came with chaos, was better than being alone. I settled for presence over peace. I mistook pain for passion.

I will never forget what I thought was the final straw. I came home one evening after visiting a friend. The moment I walked through the door, I felt something hard slam against the side of my face. Before I could process what happened, I hit the floor. My eyes opened just long enough to see his foot coming down toward me, and then everything went black.

When I woke up, I was on a stretcher. My jaw was dislocated. I had a concussion. And my soul felt fractured. When I was released from the hospital, I grabbed my child and went straight to a hotel. But here is the part we do not talk about enough: *not all support is healthy support.* Some people in my circle told me to go back. Their advice was based on fear, culture, and conditioning, not freedom. My logic and my trauma were at war. One voice said, *"You don't need him. You make the money."* The other whispered, *"At least you're not alone."* Sadly, I went back. We were bound by our brokenness.

I share this, not to sensationalize my pain, but because someone reading this might still believe they are not "in that type of relationship." I get it, I once thought the same. I did not understand that abuse does not always start with bruises; it begins with brokenness. It grows where self-worth is buried and peace is compromised.

Professional Moment

It would be incomplete, and even irresponsible, to address domestic violence without also offering psychoeducation and practical resources. If, at any point, what you read begins to feel overwhelming or triggering, pause. Set the book down. Take three slow, intentional breaths, inhaling peace and exhaling tension. Give yourself permission to step away and engage in something that soothes your emotions, a walk, prayer, music, or journaling. If you are currently in therapy, please reach out to your therapist to process your feelings or explore any unresolved pain that may surface. Healing requires gentleness with yourself; you are doing sacred work.

CYCLE OF ABUSE

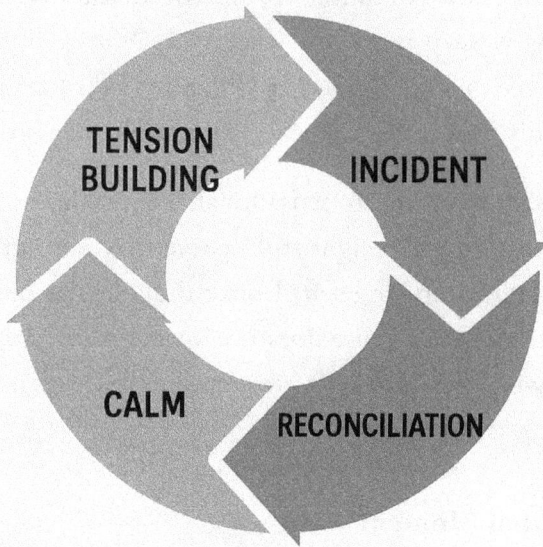

TENSION BUILDING

INCIDENT

CALM

RECONCILIATION

Domestic violence is not just about physical harm; it is about control, manipulation, and fear. It is a cycle that traps the body, mind, and soul in a silent war. The Cycle of Violence, as identified by psychologist Lenore Walker (1979), follows a repeating pattern: tension building, the explosion, and the honeymoon phase. During the tension phase, anxiety fills the home, words become sharp, and the victim walks on eggshells. The explosion follows verbal degradation, physical assault, or emotional destruction. Then comes the calm, where apologies flow, promises are made, and hope temporarily blinds reality. Over time, this cycle shortens, and the outbursts become more frequent, eroding the victim's spirit and sense of self.

Mentally, survivors often experience chronic stress, anxiety, depression, and symptoms of post-traumatic stress disorder (PTSD). The constant unpredictability creates hypervigilance, a state of being "on guard," even in safe spaces. Emotionally, victims internalize the abuse, often believing they are the problem. They begin to question their worth, their perception, and even their sanity. This psychological manipulation, known as gaslighting, distorts reality and keeps them bound in confusion (Herman, 1992). Over time, the nervous system adapts to chaos, making peace feel foreign and danger feel familiar (van der Kolk, 2014).

The body carries what the soul cannot speak. Physically, the stress of enduring abuse can manifest as headaches, fatigue, digestive issues, chronic pain, and immune system suppression. Survivors may also experience sleep disturbances, appetite changes, or even cardiovascular complications due to prolonged exposure to fear and adrenaline. As Dr. Bessel van der Kolk explains, "The body keeps the score." It remembers every threat, slap, shove, and word that pierced the heart.

There are consequences of staying. Staying in an abusive relationship has far-reaching consequences, loss of self, isolation, and increased danger. According to the National Coalition Against Domestic Violence (2022), the longer someone remains in a violent relationship, the higher the risk of severe injury or death. The abusers' control often deepens, cutting off support systems, finances, and access to help. Spiritually, the victim's view of love, self-worth, and even God can become distorted. They may begin to believe that suffering is their cross to bear. But let me be clear, God never called you to endure abuse as a demonstration of faith. He calls you to live, to be free, and to walk in peace.

Leaving is not weakness, it is deliverance. It is choosing life over survival, purpose over pain. Freedom does not mean the healing journey is easy, but it means the journey has begun. Mentally, leaving breaks the cycle of fear; emotionally, it restores clarity and self-trust; physically, it allows the body to rest and recover. Spiritually, it opens the door for God to heal what was broken. Psalm 34:18 declares, *"The Lord is close to the brokenhearted and saves those who are crushed in spirit"* *(NKJV)*. When you step out, God steps in. He replaces chaos with peace, fear with faith, and bondage with freedom.

The same God who gave you life will help you reclaim it.

Friend, if you see yourself in my story, please know this: love should never come at the cost of your safety, dignity, or soul. Healing begins the moment you acknowledge what you have been surviving. Okay, enough of the heavy. Take a minute to regroup, if needed.

If in immediate danger, dial 911. Domestic violence hotline 1-800-799-7233 or text BEGIN to 88788. The website is https://www.thehotline.org/

REFLECTIVE *Questions*

1. What emotional or spiritual attachments in your life may have begun as a connection but turned into entanglement, keeping you bound to pain, fear, or false security? What would freedom look like if you allowed God to untangle those ties?

    ....

    ....

    ....

    ....

2. In moments when you confuse attachment with love or endurance with loyalty, what truth from God's Word can help you redefine what a healthy, godly connection should look and feel like?

    ....

    ....

    ....

    ....

CHAPTER
Nine

THE SOUL CONNECTS BEYOND THE PHYSICAL

I n many church spaces, the teaching around soul-ties is reduced to sex. Yes, sexual intimacy is one of the most powerful ways a soul-tie can form, but it is not the only way. I believe part of my calling is to bridge the gap between biblical truth and psychological understanding. To teach both spiritually and naturally. You can develop a soul-tie with a parent, a best friend, a mentor, or even someone who abused you. And if you have ever felt stuck in a relationship you knew was toxic, yet could not walk away, there is a good chance a soul-tie is in play.

The healed soul must understand this: not every connection is a covenant. Not every bond is blessed. Some ties must be broken so that healing can begin. And that is what we are doing here, exposing what is hidden, naming what is real, and breaking free from what was never meant to hold you. Because healing starts when the soul is no longer bound.

Godly vs. Ungodly Soul-Ties

In my personal walk with God, my healing journey, and my professional work as a counselor, I have seen how soul-ties, both godly and ungodly, can either nourish or damage the soul. Some ties are designed by God to build us up. Others are formed through pain, sin, or trauma, and they tear us down. If you are going to pursue healing, you must learn to discern the difference.

Godly (Healthy) Soul-Ties

Godly soul-ties are formed in alignment with God's design and purpose. These ties glorify Him, promote spiritual growth, and encourage emotional and relational wholeness. When you are connected to someone through a godly soul-tie, you feel safe, emotionally, mentally, and spiritually. These relationships carry mutual respect, love, empathy, and truth. Let me be clear: Godly soul-ties are not perfect, but they are rooted in purpose, not pain.

Some Biblical examples of soul ties are:

- **Adam and God** – A spiritual bond rooted in divine intimacy and purpose.

- **Adam and Eve** – A marital bond created by God Himself to reflect unity and partnership.

- **David and Jonathan (1 Samuel 18:1-4)** – A deep friendship rooted in loyalty, sacrifice, and covenant. And no, this was not a romantic or same-sex relationship; we cannot twist Scripture to fit culture.

- **Jacob and Benjamin** – A strong familial tie born from love and loss. Jacob's bond with Benjamin was intensified by the death of his beloved wife, Rachel, during childbirth. Benjamin's name, *"son of my right hand,"* speaks to that deep connection.

- **Ruth and Naomi** – A family bond that reflected loyalty, faith, and mutual support.

- **Paul and Timothy** – A spiritual mentorship and familial bond that empowered both men in ministry.

Now that I have given biblical examples, here are a few signs of a healthy soul-tie

- You feel emotionally and mentally safe.

- You can be yourself without fear.

- The relationship fosters spiritual growth.

- There is mutual love, respect, and empathy.

- It aligns with God's Word and purpose for your life

Ungodly/Unhealthy Soul Tie

Ungodly soul-ties are birthed from brokenness, through sexual encounters outside of covenant, emotional dependency, manipulation, or trauma bonds. These connections are not led by the Spirit of God but by lust, fear, control, or unmet emotional needs. They do not lead you closer to purpose; they drain you. There is a difference between being *connected* and being *entangled.* I learned that the hard way. Some of the relationships I held onto were not built on love, trust, or mutual growth; they were built on pain, need, and brokenness. At the time, I thought the bond meant loyalty or love, but in truth, it was trauma disguised as attachment. I was tied to people not because we were good for each other, but because our wounds recognized each other. Those bonds felt familiar, even when they were harmful, because dysfunction can feel like home when you have lived in it long enough. I often say, "The soul will always seek what feels familiar until it learns what feels safe."

Professional Moment

Unhealthy bonds, whether emotional, romantic, or relational, often stem from unresolved trauma, unmet needs, or insecure attachment patterns developed early in life. Psychologically, these connections are sometimes referred to as *trauma bonds* or *codependent relationships*. They form when cycles of affection and abuse, attention and neglect, create confusion in the brain's reward system (Carnes, 1997; van der Kolk, 2014). You begin to equate inconsistency with passion, control with care, and chaos with connection. The very person who causes your pain becomes the one you turn to for relief. Professionally, we understand that the brain's chemical responses, dopamine, oxytocin, and adrenaline, reinforce these emotional highs and lows.

Spiritually, this reveals something even deeper: the enemy perverts what God designed to be pure. The soul tie, originally meant to connect us in love, covenant, and purpose, becomes contaminated by fear, dependency, and shame. Instead of bringing peace, it brings confusion. Instead of growth, it creates bondage. When you are tied to someone who feeds your weakness instead of your wholeness, your spirit becomes weary, and your peace becomes compromised. That is not love; that is captivity.

Listen, friend, in my own life, I had to face the truth: not every bond is godly just because it feels deep. Some attachments exist to teach us what we must release. I remember crying out to God, asking why breaking free hurt so badly. He gently revealed that healing requires separation, not just from people, but from patterns that keep the soul bound. He reminded me of Isaiah 61:1, *"He has sent me to bind up the brokenhearted, to proclaim freedom for the captives and release from darkness for the prisoners" (NKJV).* I realized I had been emotionally imprisoned by connections that God never authorized. Unhealthy bonds thrive on fear, fear of being alone, fear of rejection, fear of starting over. But healing requires courage. As a therapist and as a woman who has walked this road, I can say this: freedom begins when you stop confusing attachment with love. Healthy love does not require you to lose yourself. It nurtures, it empowers, and it aligns with peace.

Biblical Examples of Ungodly Soul-Ties:

- David and Bathsheba – A relationship formed in lust and deception. David was supposed to be on the battlefield, but instead pursued another man's wife.

- Samson and Delilah – A soul-tie formed with someone who did not share Samson's values or destiny. Delilah's betrayal revealed that she was only there to benefit herself.

- Tamar and Judah – A complex and painful family dynamic that led to sexual sin and generational consequences.

- Solomon and his many wives – Solomon formed ties with foreign women who turned his heart away from God, leading to idolatry and spiritual decline.

Signs of an ungodly/unhealthy soul tie

- *"That's just my friend."*

- *"We still hang out from time to time, even though we broke up."*

- *"It's just a situationship."*

- *"We have an understanding."*

- *"It's complicated."*

Sound familiar? Those phrases are often signs of emotional entanglement.

Can I say this for the ones in the back... Soul-ties can go beyond the bedroom. You may have or had

- Toxic friendships

- Church relationships

- Workplace connections

- Business partnerships

Some of these can be just as emotionally damaging as a toxic marriage/or intimate relationship:

- They drain you.

- They cross your boundaries.

- They keep you stuck in cycles of guilt, obligation, or false loyalty.

Because freedom is not just breaking ties, it is learning to form the right ones.

REFLECTION *Questions*

1. In what relationships or spaces have you mistaken depth for divine connection, holding onto bonds that felt familiar but were never fruitful? How can you begin discerning between what feeds your soul and what drains it?

   ....

   ....

   ....

   ....

2. What would it look like for you to redefine connection according to God's design, forming relationships that nurture your purpose, honor your peace, and align with His Word rather than your wounds?

   ....

   ....

   ....

   ....

Affirmation

"I am no longer bound by fear or false connection. I release every bond that was formed in brokenness and embrace divine relationships that honor my healing, my peace, and my purpose."

CHAPTER
Ten

THE WEIGHT OF A
WRONG TIE

I f you are anything like me, you probably still have questions. Even after all the research, prayer, and self-reflection, I still struggled to fully understand my own healing. On my spiritual and therapeutic journey, I began to see myself reflected in so much of what I have shared in the previous chapters. Yet, my trauma often kept me standing on the edge of confusion, wanting freedom but not quite convinced it was possible for me.

I have been hurt by people, both inside and outside of the church. I remember asking myself, *How can God heal me when some of His own people were the ones who hurt me?* There were moments when I felt unseen, unworthy, and unaccepted. Some church leaders made me feel like an outsider simply because I did not fit their mold. I did not preach like them. I did not dress like them. I acted differently. And yes, I have tattoos, so to them, I was bound for hell with gasoline drawers on. Those experiences left scars that took years to confront.

If I can be honest, it wasn't that long ago that I could have been retraumatized by those same mindsets. But God and therapy met me in that place. Through both, I found deliverance from my insecurities and the realization that God does not call the perfected; He calls the willing. I now know that He can use me, tattoos and all, *just as I am*. My healing didn't come through people's approval; it came through God's acceptance.

I needed to know more about how do I know if I have an unhealthy soul tie. And I was led to this scripture.

"For you put up with it if one brings you into bondage, if one devours you, if one takes from you, if one exalts himself, if one strikes you on the face."

2 CORINTHIANS 11:20 (NJKV).

I am going to dismantle this scripture the best way I can, that resonated with me, and prayerfully, it will help you with your deliverance.

In this verse, Paul is addressing the Corinthian church with sharp irony. He is rebuking them for tolerating abusive spiritual leaders and false teachers. Instead of rejecting exploitation, the Corinthians were putting up with it, even when it meant suffering harm. I like how Paul outlines five forms of spiritual abuse and manipulation, but these also mirror emotional and relational abuse in everyday life:

1. **"Brings you into bondage"**
   - *Spiritual Insight:* This refers to being enslaved, controlled, or manipulated. Spiritually, it's when someone dominates your faith journey instead of pointing you to Christ.

```

- *In life:* This can show up as codependent relationships, controlling friendships, or partners who manipulate through guilt, fear, or obligation.

2. **"Devours you"**

   - *Spiritually:* This implies being consumed, drained emotionally, financially, or spiritually.
   - *Relationally:* You give and give, and they keep taking your time, your peace, your energy, and sometimes your identity.

3. **"Takes from you"**

   - *Spiritually:* False leaders in Corinth were taking advantage of believers for personal gain.
   - *Professionally/Relationally:* This is exploitation, when someone uses your kindness, body, loyalty, or resources without reciprocation or respect.

4. **"Exalts himself"**

   - *Spiritually:* Prideful leadership. People use their influence not to uplift others but to elevate themselves.
   - *Personally:* Narcissistic relationships where one person constantly makes it about them, leaving no room for your voice, value, or growth.
```

5. **"Strikes you on the face"**

- *Literal and symbolic abuse.* This highlights how far manipulation can go unchecked, into verbal, emotional, or even physical abuse.

Professional Moment

From a psychological perspective, what Paul calls out is trauma bonding. We will talk more about this later in the chapter. It is the kind of unhealthy attachment that causes people to normalize abuse. Why? Because of unmet emotional needs, low self-worth, or a distorted view of love and authority.

Paul is asking a bold question here, and so am I: *Why do you tolerate what is harming you?*

I saw this scripture as an invitation to self-examination, especially if you have ever found yourself in a pattern of tolerating disrespect, manipulation, or spiritual abuse. It aligns deeply with the message I pray you will get from this book, recognizing bondage for what it is and reclaiming your worth.

Friend, I think this was the turning point for me. I finally realized I was not just hurting, I was *bound*. Bound by the kind of connections that did not bring peace, only pain. I had to be honest with myself: I had some unhealthy soul ties.

I was tired of patching my pain with temporary relief. I did not want to keep treating the symptoms; I wanted to get to the root. My trauma had become the soil where unhealthy attachments grew. And because I had not healed, I kept attracting people who were also unhealed. Let's be clear, healthy and unhealthy do not mix. Light and darkness cannot coexist. (See 2 Corinthians 6:14).

So, I had to confront what I had been avoiding: the trauma bonds I had mistaken for love, loyalty, or friendship.

Facing the Root, Healing Trauma Bonds

If you are anything like I was, you are probably wondering what a trauma bond is. Spiritually and psychologically, a *trauma bond* is a counterfeit connection. It feels deep, but it is built on shared wounds rather than shared purpose.

From a professional standpoint, trauma bonds can form in any kind of relationship, romantic, familial, platonic, workplace, or even within religious communities. They often begin in environments where love and pain coexist. According to Dr. Patrick Carnes (1997), who first defined the term, a trauma bond develops when a cycle of abuse and reward creates an emotional dependency on the very person who causes harm.

In other words, you feel "seen," but not safe. You feel "loved," but not free.

Trauma bonds often begin in childhood. When love is mixed with neglect, criticism, or abandonment, the nervous system learns that love equals instability. As adults, we unconsciously seek out people who recreate that same emotional pattern, hoping this time we can fix it or finally be chosen.

Psychologically, this is known as repetition compulsion, our subconscious's attempt to rewrite a painful story (Freud, 1920). But spiritually, it is the enemy's way of keeping us cycling in brokenness instead of walking in freedom.

Romantically, trauma bonds often begin with love bombing, overwhelming affection, constant communication, and a false sense of intimacy. In friendships, it may look like finding someone who instantly "gets you," shares similar pain, or stands by you in chaos, but subtly begins to manipulate, guilt, or control you over time.

At first, it feels comforting. Then it becomes confusing. You tell yourself, *"They need me."* Or worse, *"I need them."* But what is really happening is emotional captivity disguised as connection.

It is important to have a clear understanding of what trauma bonding looks like.

- You feel deeply connected, yet emotionally drained.

- You ignore red flags because the bond feels familiar.

- The relationship alternates between kindness and cruelty.

- You feel guilt or obligation that makes it hard to walk away.

- There's manipulation, often using guilt, past trauma, or emotional blackmail.

- They apologize, promise change, and repeat the same pattern.

Professionally speaking, this is known as intermittent reinforcement, when a person gives affection inconsistently, keeping you hooked on the hope that things will return to the "good times" (Dutton & Painter, 1981). Spiritually, it is bondage. It keeps your soul tethered to pain rather than to peace.

When Love Drains Instead of Fills

I remember being in relationships, both intimate and interpersonal, that left me completely drained. Every conversation felt heavy, every connection felt costly. What I didn't realize then was that I was living in a constant cycle of mental and emotional turmoil, mistaking exhaustion for love and chaos for connection.

I was the one who always believed I could *fix it*, fix the relationship, fix the dysfunction, fix *them*. But what it was really costing was *me*.

There was one relationship in particular where no matter what he did, I always had an excuse ready. I told myself his behavior came from his father's absence, his mother's neglect, his childhood trauma, or even "the system." I justified the pain because I confused empathy with obligation. I thought if I just loved harder, prayed more, or stayed longer, things would change.

At the time, I convinced myself this was one of my "best" relationships. Still, looking back through healed eyes, I can see it for what it really was: manipulation wrapped in affection, control disguised as love, and emotional blackmail that kept me bound.

Sometimes what we call *love* is really a trauma bond, a tie that feels familiar because it mirrors our past pain. Healing taught me that love should never drain you of your peace or cost you your identity. Real love nourishes; it doesn't deplete.

Manipulation and emotional blackmail leave wounds that do not always show on the surface, but they cut deeply into the soul. When someone uses guilt, fear, or shame to control you, it slowly chips away at your confidence, your voice, and your sense of worth. I remember the confusion, the constant questioning of myself, wondering if I was overreacting or not enough.

Emotional blackmail is subtle; it disguises itself as love, concern, or protection, but what it really does is imprison your emotions. It teaches you to please to avoid punishment, to silence your truth to keep peace, and to shrink yourself to be accepted. Over time, it is like you begin to forget who you were before the manipulation began.

Professional Moment

This relationship felt like an addiction. It was after I completed my own therapy and became a therapist that I understood that a trauma bond affects the brain's reward system. The cycle of stress and relief triggers the same chemical reactions as addiction: dopamine, cortisol, and oxytocin. You crave the connection even though it hurts you. This is why trauma bonds are often described as "soul addictions."

Trauma and manipulation can condition a person to carry guilt that was never theirs to bear. When you have lived through experiences where love was inconsistent or safety was tied to someone else's approval, you start to believe that everything that goes wrong must somehow be your fault. Manipulators reinforce that belief by twisting truth, shifting blame, and using guilt as a weapon to maintain control. Over time, the mind learns to apologize for existing, to overthink every word, and to question every emotion. You begin to feel responsible for other people's moods, reactions, and pain, while ignoring your own.

But there is something deeper at play: the longing to be understood. When someone finally "gets" your pain, it feels like home, even if that home is on fire.

I have learned that this false guilt becomes a form of bondage. Healing requires learning to separate conviction from condemnation, to know that true accountability leads to freedom, but false guilt keeps you enslaved. God never meant for you to live under the weight of shame; His truth brings clarity, not confusion, and His love silences the guilt that trauma once taught you to hold.

Yet, true love does not mirror your trauma. It heals it.

Reclaiming yourself means unlearning the lies that led you to believe love should hurt and remembering that God's love never manipulates; it liberates.

REFLECTIVE *Questions*

1. What patterns or relationships have you tolerated that drained your peace, distorted your worth, or kept you bound in confusion, and what truth is God now revealing to help you release them?

    ....

    ....

    ....

    ....

2. How has false guilt or misplaced responsibility kept you tied to people or situations God never assigned to your life? What would freedom look like if you began to see yourself through the lens of God's acceptance rather than others' approval?

    ....

    ....

    ....

    ....

CHAPTER

Eleven

WHEN YOUR PAST TRIES TO RECLAIM YOU

M arried in what I call the healthiest relationship I have ever had. But wait, the past started haunting me. In my dreams, my thoughts, during intimate times with my husband. I was acting out, not so much my trauma but my soul ties.

I thought the vows, the dress, and the ceremony were the beginning of a new story, but in reality, I had never closed the last chapter. My heart said "yes" to my husband, but parts of my soul were still bound to relationships that had long ended, relationships that had imprinted pain, fear, and mistrust into my emotional DNA. These were not just memories; they were soul ties, unseen cords linking me to experiences and people who no longer deserved a place in my life. Little did I know that they all walked down the aisle with me as well.

I entered my marriage believing I was ready, but my reactions revealed otherwise. Whenever my husband didn't respond the way I wanted, old wounds whispered, *You're not safe*. When he tried to love me, I questioned his motives. My mind said, "I trust you," but my soul said, "Prepare to be abandoned."

You see, those old soul ties carried remnants of rejection, comparison, and fear. I did not realize I had made silent vows that shaped my behavior, vows like *"I'll never let a man hurt me again"* or *"I'll always be in control."* Those vows became walls, and while they kept pain out, they also kept love from coming in. Marriage requires vulnerability, but how can you be vulnerable when your soul is divided? My husband was loving me in the present, but I was still arguing with ghosts from my past. The enemy of my soul wanted to keep me fragmented, because a divided heart cannot love wholly.

Professionally, I can identify this as *emotional displacement*, projecting unresolved feelings from one relationship onto another (Johnson, 2015). Spiritually, it was a battle between my healed identity in Christ and the remnants of my wounded soul.

When The Body Speaks

I knew I needed to heal from my wounds, but I didn't realize just how deeply those wounds had rooted themselves in every part of my life. What I did not know was how every emotional connection, every sexual encounter, both the ones I chose and the ones that were forced upon me, would follow me into my marriage. It affected the way I saw my husband, our intimacy, and our emotional connection. What made it harder was that I was still holding on to secrets. I could talk about my relationships, my childhood, even my family drama, but I never talked about my body being violated. Some of those memories were buried so deep that I honestly forgot about them, but my body had not. My body remembered what my mind tried to forget. My behavior remembered how to respond, even when I couldn't explain why.

It was not until I was pregnant with my third child that everything started to surface. Therapy with Faye helped me to understand that the emotional stress of that pregnancy began to stir up what I had suppressed for years. I was being triggered, and the floodgates of old pain began to open. I remember being four months pregnant when I started feeling contractions. They rushed me in for an emergency appointment, and that moment changed everything. The doctor said I might be having a uterine abruption. He spoke with no compassion, no sense of care, just cold facts. I will never forget how he turned to my husband and said, "There's a possibility she could hemorrhage to death, and you'll need to decide and sign paperwork on who we should resuscitate." Those words pierced me. The rest of that day is still a blur. I was placed on bed rest with two small children at home and a husband in the Navy who was constantly going back and forth out to sea.

But let me pause right there, I will not leave you hanging. By the grace of God, we made it. Our daughter made it. She spent time in the NICU, but she fought through, and today she is everything they said she would never be.

That experience changed me. It opened my eyes to how stress and trauma live in the body. That pregnancy was the beginning of my true healing journey. I remember one night in prayer when God whispered to me, *"You're not fighting your husband; you're fighting your history."* That truth broke me. Every time I withdrew emotionally, it was not because of him; it was because my soul was still trying to unlearn patterns of self-protection that once kept me alive. I began to understand why I locked the bedroom door at night and why I needed a light on, even with my husband lying next to me. It was not that I did not feel safe with him; it was that I needed to feel in control. Those small actions were my way of protecting myself; they were my signal that if someone came in, I would have time to hide or defend myself.

Through therapy and honesty, I finally had the language to explain why certain touches triggered memories, so I shared about the molestation and attempted rape. I could tell him, "This is why I react the way I do," instead of pushing him away and leaving him confused. He no longer had to wonder if something was wrong with him. It wasn't him, it was me. I was wrestling with regret, guilt, insecurity, and a deep loss of self-respect. I was emotionally starved, what I now call emotional anorexia, because for so long I had denied myself the nourishment of safety, love, and truth.

That pregnancy did not just birth a child; it birthed my healing.

The Unseen Strings

That is my story. And I know I am not the only one. Let us be honest, not everyone practiced abstinence before marriage. And because we did not, some of us are still holding onto the memories of how others made us feel. Many who struggle with soul ties find themselves unconsciously comparing their current marriage or relationship to a past experience with someone they were once intimate with.

The soul keeps receipts. It remembers the moments, the emotions, the touch, the words. Before we know it, we are thinking, *"So-and-so used to kiss me like this… he or she used to hold me like that."* And we wonder why we can't seem to fully connect with our spouse; it is because, emotionally, there are other people standing in the way. When the soul is entangled with past partners, you bring spiritual residue into a sacred covenant. What God designed to be pure becomes polluted by unresolved emotional debris.

Many of the soul wounds we wrestle with are the result of giving someone else the kind of allegiance that belongs only to Jesus. God never intended for our hearts to be divided. That's why there are consequences when we attach ourselves outside His design for intimacy.

Sexual intimacy was designed by God to create unity, not confusion. Scripture says in *Genesis 2:24*, "Therefore a man shall leave his father and mother and be joined to his wife, and they shall become one flesh" (NKJV). That verse is more than poetic; it is a spiritual, psychological, and physiological truth. When two people engage in sexual intimacy, something far deeper than the body connects. The soul, our emotional, mental, and spiritual essence, forms a bond that can outlast the relationship itself. This is why even after a breakup, individuals often find themselves thinking about or emotionally comparing their current partner to someone from the past.

Professional Moment

The body's biochemistry contributes to this attachment. During sexual activity, the brain releases powerful bonding hormones, oxytocin (known as the "love" or "trust" hormone) and dopamine (the pleasure and reward neurotransmitter). According to McIlhaney and Bush (2008) in *Hooked: New Science on How Casual Sex Is Affecting Our Children*, these neurochemicals reinforce emotional attachment and connection, making it neurologically difficult to "detach" once that bond has been formed. This process does not discriminate between healthy or unhealthy relationships; the brain bonds regardless of context.

When those connections are not surrendered or healed, remnants of that emotional and spiritual tie can intrude into new relationships. The mind recalls familiar sensations, emotional responses, and even unspoken expectations linked to the previous partner. These memories can create emotional interference, leading individuals to compare their current partner's affection, intimacy, or behavior to someone from the past. According to Dr. Patrick Carnes (2012), author of *Out of the Shadows: Understanding Sexual Addiction*, unresolved sexual attachments can distort intimacy, causing emotional confusion and relational dissatisfaction.

Spiritually speaking, these lingering attachments become soul echoes, resonances of a bond that has not been broken. When the past is not surrendered to God, it can show up uninvited in the present. We may find ourselves reminiscing about a moment, a touch, or a feeling tied to someone else, not realizing that this is the residue of an unhealed connection. These unbroken ties can hinder us from fully experiencing the emotional and spiritual oneness that God intends within our current covenant relationship.

Healing begins when we invite God into those hidden places. As 2 Corinthians 10:5 reminds us, we must "cast down arguments and every high thing that exalts itself against the knowledge of God, bringing every thought into captivity to the obedience of Christ" (NKJV). Through prayer, counseling, and intentional emotional work, we can identify those lingering ties, confront the false narratives they create, and release them. Forgiveness and repentance break the spiritual agreement that keeps us bound. Professional therapy helps us name and process the attachment, while spiritual surrender allows us to walk in freedom.

Living free from past sexual bonds does not mean we erase memory; it means we redeem the meaning of those experiences through truth, accountability, and divine healing. When we release what no longer serves us, our hearts and minds become fully available to experience love in its purest form, the way God designed it to be.

I was finally living whole in my marriage. As I healed, my marriage began to breathe. My husband was no longer fighting for a place against my past; he was walking beside a woman who was learning to live free. The more I released, the more room I made for love.

Marriage became the mirror God used to show me the unhealed parts of my soul. And rather than resist the reflection, I leaned into grace. The truth is, love requires healing, and healing requires truth. When the two meet, wholeness begins.

Today, I can confidently say that what once hindered me has now helped me. The pain that once divided my soul has become the testimony that unites others to their own healing.

REFLECTION *Questions*

1. What parts of your past still echo in your present, memories, emotions, or silent vows that continue to shape how you love, trust, or respond in your current relationships? What would it look like to invite God into those places and finally close that chapter?

    ....

    ....

    ....

    ....

2. How has your body or behavior been communicating unhealed pain from your past? In what ways can prayer, therapy, and vulnerability become tools to help your soul and body align with the freedom God designed for you to live in?

    ....

    ....

    ....

    ....

PRAYER FOR
Release

Father,

*I thank You for revealing the hidden ties of my soul.
Today, I surrender every connection that has kept me
bound to my past. I release the pain, the memories,
and the fear. Heal my heart, restore my identity, and
teach me to love from a whole place.
Where my soul has been divided, make me one
again, with You and with the person You have joined
me to.
In Jesus' name, amen.*

CHAPTER
Twelve

THE NIGHT GOD
MADE ME WHOLE

The enemy can set the stage, but God always provides a way out (1 Corinthians 10:13). The question is, will we take it? Freedom is not just about letting go; it is about healing through it and being delivered from what once held us captive.

Where thoughts go, energy flows. What you focus on grows. Philippians 4:8 reminds us to think on what is true, noble, and praiseworthy (NKJV). This is not just spiritual advice; it is psychological truth. Redirecting your thoughts helps renew your neural pathways (Doidge, 2007), allowing your mind to align with God's truth rather than trauma's lies.

Breaking a soul tie requires spiritual and psychological work. Begin with repentance and confession, acknowledge any sin, especially sexual sin, and ask for God's forgiveness. Then move to renunciation, declaring your intention to sever that connection in your mind, heart, and spirit. Finally, focus on ongoing healing through prayer, Scripture, worship, and professional guidance.

Remember, freedom is both a moment and a maintenance plan.

My Path to Wholeness

There came a moment when my husband and I could no longer live divided between our past and our purpose. We both knew that pieces of our hearts were still tethered to places and people God had already called us out of. We repented, prayed, and asked the Lord to deliver us from every soul tie, both the ones formed through sin and the ones formed through suffering.

I will never forget what my deliverance looked like. God met me in a dream. In the dream, I was standing on the edge of a cliff. Before me stood the faces of those who had taken something from me, the ones who stole my innocence, the ones who assaulted me, and even the ones I gave myself to in search of love. I watched as each one turned to look at me, and one by one, they began to fall off the cliff. I did not push them. I did not chase them. I just stood there, and as they disappeared into the distance, I felt something break, something I had carried for years.

When I looked down at myself, I realized something had changed. I did not look the same. The holes that once symbolized my brokenness, shame, and guilt were gone. My body looked whole. My soul felt light. For the first time in my life, I did not feel used or incomplete; I felt redeemed.

When I woke up, tears streamed down my face. I knew, without question, that God had delivered me. Every invisible chain that once tied me to pain, trauma, and regret had been severed. Later that morning, my husband shared that he, too, had a dream that night. His dream mirrored mine. It was confirmation that God had not only restored me but had healed *us*.

God is still a Deliverer. He did not just free me from people, He freed me from torment, from emotional captivity, and from the lie that someone else still had control over my peace or my body. Deliverance, I learned, is not always dramatic. Sometimes it is silent. Sometimes it is holy, still, and deeply personal. It is when heaven touches the wounds that hell once claimed.

That night, I did not just dream; I was redeemed.

You, too, can reclaim your soul by breaking soul ties. The first thing you have to do is identify dysfunctional and unhealthy soul ties. Unhealthy soul ties keep you from finding and understanding the truth of who you are. They keep you tied to confusion, fear, and emotional unrest. You end up fanning the flames of anger, bitterness, and resentment, only to realize you are the one being burned.

Friend, if you are struggling to recognize these patterns, I encourage you to document them or discuss them openly with a trusted therapist or spiritual advisor. Journaling and therapeutic dialogue can uncover blind spots and help bring what has been hidden into the light.

Professional Moment

As a therapist, I have come to understand that spiritual deliverance and psychological healing often work hand in hand. What God revealed to me through that dream aligns with what trauma experts describe as the process of *integration*, when the fragmented parts of the self begin to reconnect through awareness, forgiveness, and release (van der Kolk, 2014).

Trauma, especially sexual trauma, creates invisible attachments that live in both the mind and the body. Survivors often internalize shame and self-blame, believing their worth was diminished by what happened to them (Herman, 2015). Healing, however, comes through reclaiming ownership of the self, physically, emotionally, and spiritually.

From a clinical perspective, releasing soul ties mirrors the process of releasing trauma bonds. These are emotional attachments formed through cycles of abuse, control, or dependency (Carnes, 2019). Healing requires both divine deliverance and psychological awareness. One without the other leaves the soul only partially restored.

That night, God used the language of my subconscious, a dream, to help my body release what my mind had carried for too long. The symbolic act of seeing those faces fall away was my psyche and my spirit coming into agreement: I no longer belonged to pain.

Spiritually, there is a difference between forgiveness and freedom. Forgiveness releases others, but freedom releases *you*. My dream was God's way of showing me that deliverance does not erase the memory; it removes the sting. Scripture reminds us in John 8:36 (NKJV), *"Therefore if the Son makes you free, you shall be free indeed."* That word *indeed* means *truly, completely, without condition.* God doesn't just offer partial deliverance; He restores entirely.

I also think of Psalm 34:4, which says, *"I sought the Lord, and He heard me, and delivered me from all my fears."* Deliverance is not only from demonic oppression; it is also from emotional oppression, the fear, shame, and spiritual residue that keep us bound.

That night was not just a spiritual event; it was a spiritual surgery. God closed the open wounds in my soul. He did not just mend me; He made me new.

Maintaining Your Victory

Once you acknowledge that the dynamics are unhealthy, maintaining your freedom becomes a daily decision. Healing does not just happen; it is cultivated, and that deliverance is a divine act, but maintaining freedom requires daily partnership with God.

Here are practical and spiritual ways to remain whole:

1. **Acknowledge the Bond:**

   Be honest about the connection. Name it. Write it down. Who or what are you still attached to?

2. **Repent and Renounce:**

   Repent for the agreement you made in that connection. Even if you were unaware, renounce the tie spiritually.

3. **Renew Your Mind:**

   Be intentional about replacing old thoughts with God's truth (Romans 12:2). Healing the mind reinforces what deliverance begins.

4. **Change Your Daily Routine**

   If your life still revolves around reminders of the person or situation, healing will be harder. Begin to shift your habits intentionally, but gently. You do not have to overhaul everything overnight. Focus on small, positive changes that help you rebuild your sense of self.

5. **Allow Yourself to Grieve**

   Ending an unhealthy connection is still a loss. You may grieve what you hoped would be more than what it actually was. Ambiguous loss, a term coined by Pauline Boss (2000), describes the pain of losing something that was never fully clear or complete. Give yourself permission to mourn what was and release what cannot be.

6. **Practice Intentional Self-Compassion**

You may feel ashamed, angry, or embarrassed that you stayed as long as you did. Be kind to yourself. Everyone struggles with unhealthy attachments at some point. Self-compassion, according to Neff (2021), involves treating yourself with the same grace you would offer a friend. You are not your past choices; you are a soul in process.

7. **Establish Boundaries:**

Emotional and spiritual boundaries protect your wholeness. Boundaries are not barriers; they are gates of wisdom (Cloud & Townsend, 2017).

8. **Stay Accountable:**

Continue therapy, mentorship, or counseling with trusted spiritual and clinical professionals. Freedom grows in community.

9. **Develop a Support System**

Surround yourself with people who support your healing. This may mean leaving your comfort zone to meet new people or joining a faith-based or therapeutic support group. The goal is to stay connected, because isolation fuels relapse into old patterns (Cloud & Townsend, 2017).

10. Practice Self-Care

Rest, nourish your body, and prioritize emotional and spiritual care. Remember, self-care is not selfish; it is stewardship.

11. Guard Your Spirit:

Be mindful of what and who you entertain. Old habits and connections can attempt to reopen what God has healed.

12. Celebrate Your Healing:

Each time you feel peace in a place that used to hurt, acknowledge it. Gratitude reinforces transformation.

A Prayer to break soul ties

Heavenly Father, I come before You with a heart ready to heal. I acknowledge that I have formed connections that were not Your will. Right now, I surrender those ties to You. I repent for every agreement I made that allowed that bond to take root. In the name of Jesus, I break and renounce every ungodly soul-tie. I sever every spiritual, emotional, and mental chain that binds me to that person. I choose freedom. I release them, and I bless them. Fill every empty place in me with Your presence, Your love, and Your truth. Help me walk forward in wholeness, identity, and peace. I am Yours, and I declare that no one and nothing has power over my soul but You. In Jesus' name, Amen.

From Ruins to Redemption

When we form soul-ties, especially ungodly ones, they often reflect how we see ourselves. If you believe you are unworthy of real love, you will settle for crumbs. If you think you have to earn love, you will perform. If you confuse pain for passion, you will cling to chaos.

That is why healing your self-worth is not optional; it is foundational. You must unlearn the lies:

- *That you are only valuable when someone wants you.*

- *That staying loyal to dysfunction is a sign of strength.*

- *That being alone means being abandoned.*

Self-worth is restored when you start seeing yourself through God's eyes, not the eyes of those who mishandled you. You are not disposable. You are not broken beyond repair. You are not who you were when you made those decisions.

One of the most damaging effects of a soul-tie is that it can strip you of your identity. You start to lose sight of who you are because so much of your emotional energy has been invested in someone else. You lose your voice. Your vision. Your values.

But the good news is, identity can be reclaimed.

In Christ, you are:

- Chosen (1 Peter 2:9)

- Loved (Romans 8:38-39)

- Whole (Colossians 2:10)

- Forgiven (Ephesians 1:7)

- Free (Galatians 5:1)

Reclaiming your identity means:

- Rediscovering your voice without fear.

- Defining your values without guilt.

- Setting new standards without apology.

- Walking in your purpose without shame.

Friend, here are some practical steps to rebuild:

Breaking a soul-tie is powerful, but it is just the beginning. Once you have severed the unhealthy bond, the real work begins: rebuilding your soul. You have emptied the space; now you have to refill it with truth, identity, and purpose. Otherwise, you risk going right back to the very thing that broke you. This part of the journey is sacred. It is where the pieces of you that were scattered through trauma, heartbreak, and codependency are gathered, restored, and redefined. This is the heart of healing.

1. **Re-establish Boundaries:**

   Create space for healing. Don't entertain texts, calls, or messages from old ties. Closure isn't a conversation; it's a commitment.

2. **Immerse in the Word of God:**

   You can't heal your identity without the One who gave it to you. Read Scripture daily to renew your mind.

3. **Do the Inner Work:**

   Journal, reflect, get therapy or coaching. Ask yourself: *What made me stay? What did I believe about myself that allowed that bond to form?*

4. **Surround Yourself with Truth-Tellers:**

   Build community with people who will remind you who you are in God, not who you were in your brokenness.

5. **Reignite Your Purpose:**

   Return to the dreams and passions you once put on hold for that relationship. God did not cancel your calling just because you got detoured.

Healing does not just mean breaking free; it means building something better in its place. Friend, remember the healed soul does not go back. The healed soul rises, rebuilds, and reclaims everything the enemy tried to use for destruction, and gives God the glory for the restoration.

Meditate on these verses to anchor your soul in truth:

- Romans 8:1 — You are not condemned.

- 2 Corinthians 5:17 — You are a new creation.

- Galatians 5:1 — You are called to freedom.

A PRAYER *for* *Rebuilding*

Father,

I thank You that breaking the tie was only the beginning. Now, I ask for your help to rebuild what was lost. Restore my identity. Heal my self-worth. Fill the places in me that were emptied by false love and misplaced loyalty. Remind me of who I am in You. Give me the strength to walk forward with confidence, peace, and clarity. I no longer carry the weight of what broke me. I walk in the freedom and fullness of who You've called me to be.
In Jesus' name, Amen.

REFLECTION *Questions*

1. What areas of your heart or mind still feel tethered to past pain, shame, or false identity, and how might you begin to invite God's truth and grace into those spaces so that healing becomes complete, not partial?

    ....

    ....

    ....

    ....

2. Now that you understand freedom is both a moment and a maintenance plan, what daily practices, spiritual, emotional, or relational, can help you protect your wholeness and walk confidently in your restored identity?

    ....

    ....

    ....

    ....

From Broken to Golden

As I close these pages, I can finally say with peace in my heart, my journey was worth it. Every broken relationship, every tear-stained pillow, every sleepless night, and every misstep led me right into the arms of a God who never let me go. What once felt like punishment, I now see as preparation. What once felt like loss, I now recognize as grace in disguise.

I am a living witness that God restores what's been shattered and redeems what's been lost. I don't just exist as a survivor, I *stand* as evidence of His goodness and His relentless love. Through every season, He has proven Himself faithful.

My healing journey reminds me of *Kintsugi*, the ancient Japanese art of repairing broken pottery with lacquer mixed with gold, silver, or platinum. This technique, also called *Kintsukuroi*, meaning "golden repair", doesn't hide the cracks; it honors them. The broken places become lined with gold, and the once-fractured vessel becomes more beautiful, more valuable, and stronger than before.

That's what God did for me. He didn't discard my broken pieces; He redeemed them. He mended my soul with mercy and sealed the fractures with grace. Each golden seam tells a story: of pain transformed, of trauma healed, of a woman made whole again.

I went from broken to golden. And I pray, as you've journeyed through these pages, that you, too, begin to see the beauty in your own restoration. May this book remind you that your story isn't over; it's being rewritten by the hands of a faithful God.

May you find peace in the process, healing in His presence, and purpose in every scar. You are not forgotten, you are not too far gone, and you are most certainly not broken beyond repair.

My Final Declaration: I Am the Healed Soul

I stand today as a woman who has walked through fire and found gold in the ashes. I am no longer defined by what broke me, but by the One who rebuilt me. My story is not one of shame; it is one of grace, redemption, and purpose.

I am the healed soul.

I am the woman who faced her pain, confronted her truth, and allowed God to write beauty into the broken lines of her story. I am whole, not because life has been perfect, but because God met me in the cracks and filled them with His light.

I no longer chase validation, because I've found identity. I no longer live from wounds, but from wisdom. I no longer hide the scars; they are evidence that I survived, that I healed, and that I am free.

Every tear I cried became water for the seeds of my destiny. Every setback became a setup for purpose. Every chapter of pain became a paragraph of praise. I now carry peace where fear once lived and love where shame once ruled.

So, this is my declaration:

I am restored.

I am redeemed.

I am renewed.

I am the healed soul.

And as you close this book, I pray you find yourself whispering the same words, not as a hope, but as a truth waiting to be lived:

"I am the healed soul."

Friend, when you have done the work, you deserve to declare

I Am the Healed Soul

Today, I choose healing.
Today, I choose peace.
Today, I release what broke me and embrace what built me.

I am not what happened to me.
I am not the mistakes I made.
I am not the words that wounded me.
I am who God says I am, whole, loved, and enough.

CHAPTER TWELVE

Every piece of me that was once shattered
has been touched by grace.
My pain has purpose.
My past has power.
My story carries healing for someone else.

I no longer walk with my head bowed in shame,
I lift it in **victory.**
I no longer live in fear,
I live in **freedom.**
I no longer hide my scars,
I wear them as proof that **I am still here, still breathing, still chosen.**

God has taken what was broken and made it beautiful.
He has filled every empty place with **peace,**
every hollow space with **hope,**
and every scar with **strength.**

So I declare, with confidence and faith:

I am restored.

I am redeemed.

I am renewed.

I am the Healed Soul.

REFERENCES

- American Psychological Association. (2023). "Blended families: Supporting mental health in complex homes."

- American Psychiatric Association. (2022). *Diagnostic and statistical manual of mental disorders* (5th-TR). American Psychiatric Association. https://doi.org/10.1176/appi.books.9780890425787

- Ainsworth, M. D. S., Blehar, M. C., Waters, E., & Wall, S. (1978). *Patterns of attachment: A psychological study of the strange situation.* Lawrence Erlbaum.

- Boss, P. (2000). *Ambiguous Loss: Learning to Live with Unresolved Grief.* Harvard University Press.

- Bowlby, J. (1988). *A Secure Base: Parent-Child Attachment and Healthy Human Development.* Basic Books.

- Carnes, P. (1997). *The Betrayal Bond: Breaking Free of Exploitive Relationships.* Health Communications, Inc.

- Carnes, P. (2012). *Out of the Shadows: Understanding Sexual Addiction* (3rd ed.). Hazelden Publishing.

- Chen, A. (2019). *The Attachment Theory Workbook: Powerful Tools to Promote Understanding, Increase Stability & Build Lasting Relationships.* Althea Press.

- Cloud, H., & Townsend, J. (2017). *Boundaries: When to Say Yes, How to Say No to Take Control of Your Life.* Zondervan.

- Cruz, D., Lichten, M., Berg, K., & George, P. (2022). Developmental trauma: Conceptual framework, associated risks and comorbidities, and evaluation and treatment. *Frontiers in Psychiatry, 13*, 800687. https://doi.org/10.3389/fpsyt.2022.800687

- Doidge, N. (2007). *The Brain That Changes Itself: Stories of Personal Triumph from the Frontiers of Brain Science.* Viking.

- Dutton, D. G., & Painter, S. L. (1981). Traumatic Bonding: The Development of Emotional Attachments in Battered Women and Other Relationships of Intermittent Abuse. *Victimology: An International Journal, 6*(1-4), 139–155.

- Evans, J. (2019). *Marriage on the Rock: 25th Anniversary Edition.* XO Publishing.

- Feldman, R. (2017). *The Neurobiology of Human Attachments. Trends in Cognitive Sciences,* 21(2), 80–99.

- Freud, S. (1920). *Beyond the Pleasure Principle.* Standard Edition, Vol. 18.

- Ganong, L. H., & Coleman, M. (2017). *Stepfamily Relationships: Development, Dynamics, and Interventions.* Springer.

- Helmstetter, S. (2019). *Negative self-talk and how to change it.* Park Avenue Press.

- Herman, J. L. (1992). *Trauma and Recovery: The Aftermath of Violence, from Domestic Abuse to Political Terror.* Basic Books.

- Life Application Study Bible, *King James Version.* (2017). Tyndale.

- McLeod, S., (2013). Psychosocial Stages. Erik Erikson. Retrieved from https://www.simplypsychology.org/simplypsychology.org-Erik-Erikson.pdf

- McIlhaney, J. S., & Bush, F. (2008). *Hooked: New Science on How Casual Sex Is Affecting Our Children.* Northfield Publishing.

- National Coalition Against Domestic Violence. (2022). *Statistics and Facts on Domestic Violence.* www.ncadv.org

- NIV – *Scripture quotations taken from the Holy Bible, New International Version®, NIV®. Copyright © 1973, 1978, 1984, 2011 by Biblica, Inc.™ Used by permission. All rights reserved worldwide.*

- NKJV – *Scripture quotations taken from the New King James Version®. Copyright © 1982 by Thomas Nelson. Used by permission. All rights reserved.*

- Pychyl, T. A., & Sirois, F. M. (2016). Procrastination, Emotion Regulation, and Well-being. In S. S. Oxford Handbook of Emotion, Social Cognition, and Problem Solving in Adulthood.

- Van der Kolk, B. (2014). *The Body Keeps the Score: Brain, Mind, and Body in the Healing of Trauma.* Penguin Books.

- Wiest, B. (2020). *The mountain is you: Transforming self-sabotage into self-mastery.* Thought Catalog Books.

THE HEALED SOUL

ACKNOWLEDGEMENTS

To Dorothy Moore and N. Faye Joseph, thank you. Each of you played a profound and intimate role in my healing journey.

Faye, you were the first to show me that my voice mattered. You equipped me with the tools and language I needed to begin healing, truly healing, from the inside out.

Dorothy, my *"Thread Puller,"* you gently guided me to speak from my inner truth rather than my emotions. You created a safe space for me to unravel, reflect, and rebuild. You challenged me to stop focusing on what "they" did or failed to do, and instead to heal from where I stand today. For that, I say thank you.

To my family, friends, and church family who walked beside me throughout this journey—holding me accountable when I needed structure and comforting me when I needed grace—I am forever grateful.

www.ingramcontent.com/pod-product-compliance
Lightning Source LLC
Chambersburg PA
CBHW060229030426
42335CB00014B/1379